A RESOUNDING FAILURE:
MARTIN AND THE FRENCH IN SIAM
1672–1693

The great pagoda at Ayutthaya, from
Tachard's Voyage de Siam . . . , *1686*

A RESOUNDING FAILURE:
MARTIN AND THE FRENCH IN SIAM
1672–1693

by

MICHAEL SMITHIES

SILKWORM BOOKS
CHIANG MAI

Some other books by Michael Smithies

Chaumont and Choisy: Aspects of the Embassy to Siam 1685
The Siamese Memoirs of Count Claude de Forbin 1685–1688
Alexander Hamilton: A Scottish Sea Captain in Southeast Asia 1689–1723
Abbé de Choisy: Journal of a Voyage to Siam, 1685–1686
The Discourses at Versailles of the First Siamese Ambassadors to France
The Siamese Embassy to the Sun King: The Personal Memoirs of Kosa Pan

***

First published in 1998 by
Silkworm Books
54/1 Sridonchai Road, Chiang Mai 50100, Thailand.
E-mail: silkworm@pobox.com

Set in 11 pt. Garamond
Cover design by T. Jittidejarak
Front cover: Cross-section of the *Ecueil*, a ship in the Duquesne-Guiton fleet in
1690–1691, adapted from Sottas's *Histoire de la Compagnie royale des Indes*
orientales, 1164–1719
End papers: The cathedral at Pondichéry in the early eighteenth century
Drawing by Jacques Dumarçay

Printed by O.S. Printing House, Bangkok.

CONTENTS

v

ILLUSTRATIONS

European horseman in 17th-century dress
Wat Suwannaram, Thonburi, 19th century
Reproduced, by permission, from M. Sportès, *Ombres Siamoises.*

PREFACE

THE violent change of government which occurred in Lopburi in May 1688 was not unexpected. François Martin, the head of the French factory in Pondichéry, was probably not alone in predicting it. But, without being directly involved, in General Desfarges' absurd expedition to Phuket, Martin had almost a ringside seat to the events which unfurled in Siam, even if the delays in receiving the 'packets' (of letters) giving him all the details were often considerable. He received, too, verbatim reports from key players in these happenings, including Samuel White and de Bruant on the two Mergui disasters; Desfarges, de Vertesalles, and others on events in Bangkok; Forbin on the first French embassy to Siam; and Céberet on the second. Martin was uniquely privileged in this respect.

These usually clearly written memoirs have only once been published before in French, more than sixty years ago, and are now for the most part unobtainable. All references to Siam have been extracted and translated here, and are placed in their general context. After completing this translation of the references to Siam in Martin's *Mémoires*, I accidentally learnt that there exists a complete English translation of the memoirs, sponsored by the Indian Council of Historical Research, published between 1981 and 1990. I have not had access to this, unfortunately.

My thanks go, as ever, to two persons who have continued to help me in my work: Dirk van der Cruysse for first indicating the rich mine of information concerning the French in Siam between 1685 and 1688 to be found in François Martin's memoirs, and to Jacques Dumarçay for managing to procure for me an uncut copy of this rarest of works, the three volumes of the only French edition (1931–1934) of these memoirs.

I am grateful, too, to my publisher, Trasvin Jittidejarak, for agreeing to undertake publication of this work and so allow an English-reading public to gain further insights into the kaleidoscope of events in Ayutthaya, Lopburi, Bangkok, and Mergui in the years leading up to and immediately after the revolution of 1688, or as we prefer to call it, the *coup d'état*.

Footnotes have been avoided in this edition. Instead, explanatory comments are incorporated into the text.

Michael Smithies

April 1997
Bua Yai, Korat

King Narai observing a lunar eclipse with Jesuits, Lopburi,
11 December 1685
From Tachard's, *Voyage de Siam . . . ,* 1686.

Pondichéry cathedral today
Photograph by Jacques Dumarçay

INTRODUCTION

FRANÇOIS MARTIN AND PONDICHÉRY

ALMOST nothing is known about the early life of François Martin (1634–1706), the founder of the French trading post of Pondichéry on the Coromandel coast, other than what the garrulous sceptic and ship scrivener Robert Challe tells us in his *Journal d'un voyage fait aux Indes Orientales (1690–1691)*. Challe (1659–1721), who may have been distantly related to Martin, wrote:

> Monsieur Martin is a Parisian, the natural son of an important wholesale grocer in the Halles. His father, immensely rich, gave him a very good education in trade, and wanted to make a merchant of him. But his sudden death prevented him from writing his will or from giving any benefit to his son. His half-brother, the only legitimate child of the grocer, having even in the lifetime of his father purchased the position of treasurer to the military messing commission, showed him the door, unwilling to give him any portion of a very fine inheritance, even though he was less legitimate than his half-brother [François Martin], his mother having been the subject of very untoward reports, and it being publicly stated in the Halles that the father's son was being driven out so that the mother's bastard could inherit...
>
> The death of his father took away any hope of being set up and only gave him, as inheritance, the name of Martin, which belonged to him, and which he shared with another to whom perhaps it did

not belong. Whatever the case, not knowing what to do, and completely without resources, having always been scrupulously faithful to his father and too upright a person to profit on his own account, he was reduced to becoming a shop assistant with another grocer, and was still such when aged between twenty-eight and twenty-nine years, he married, twelve years after the death of his father.

He had fallen in love with the daughter of a fishwife, otherwise a dealer in fish, who had also fallen in love with him. Things progressed smoothly, her petticoats increased in girth, and he married her. But her mother, after she married, neither wished to hear speak of her daughter nor her son-in-law, and showed both of them the door. The merchant where he worked, not wishing to have a married shop assistant, dismissed him. So he lived for two years and more with his wife in perfect union, but severely constrained by necessity, the more so as the improvements they could gain were very small, for want of patronage rather than wit...

Finally, reduced to despair, and unable to tolerate so miserable an existence, he presented himself to the gentlemen of the [French] Indies Company; and as he had as much intelligence as a man can have and he understood perfectly the exchange and re-exchange of bills, calculations and stock lists, he was taken on to keep them for double entry bookkeeping. It was in this way that he left for the Indies. The famous Marcara and Caron profitably made use of his services in in Surat, Masulipatam, Bengal, and in all the other places in the Indies where the Company's commerce then flourished after being established under the auspices of the late Jean-Baptiste Colbert...

The different voyages which Mr Martin was obliged to take by sea, and the activities in which he was involved, gave lustre as much to his bravery and his intrepidity as to his prudent management as seen in his accounts and his trading. The Company, very pleased with his services, raised him by degrees, until he finally became the governor-general of the French in the Indies...(1979, 381–2)

Before continuing with Challe's account (in which the most romantic part is yet to come), it should perhaps be mentioned here that Martin sought letters of legitimization when he was nineteen years old, and the act drawn up specified that he was the natural son of "Gilles Martin, of our good city of Paris, and of Péronne Gosselin, then free and not married". In other words, he was a natural child but not an adulterous child. The act also mentions he was given an excellent education in trade, as well as "good fare, care and instruction." But for some reason, possibly the death of his father, these 'letters of legitimization' of 1653 were not registered, as required, within one year of being drawn up, and were only finally presented in 1658. His half-brother may have been born after him.

Let Challe resume:

> Mr Martin had many times requested to the gentlemen of the Company a successor and his recall; but, he being too necessary to them, he had not managed to obtain one or the other. He was loath to publicize his birth and his marriage, but finally the love he maintained, and still maintains, for his wife, and his affection as a good father for his children forced him into an elucidation. He hoped to return to his country and the bosom of his family to enjoy the fruits of his labours in the Indies, but seeing it was impossible, he revealed his story himself to the Company and requested the alternative: either to let him return to Europe, or to send him his wife and his children...
>
> It was twenty-two years and more since he had left without bidding farewell to his wife and without saying where he was going; who, in a word, he had abandoned, and since that time no news had been received by either party. He did not know if she was dead or alive; he could not even give any identifying mark by which she could be recognized except the street and the house in which she was living when he left. But, after so many years, the owners of the house had changed, and there had been so many different tenants that no one had any knowledge of her. All trace of what had

become of her was lost. Those who had been offered a considerable reward for this enquiry, after six weeks of useless searching, were ready to abandon the enterprise when pure chance allowed them to find in a moment what they had sought for so long.

Passing by a street near the Halles, they heard someone call 'Madame Martin'. They turned around, and saw that the Mme Martin who was being called had in front of her her stock tray in which she was carrying carps and eels, just like any of the retail fishwives who go all over Paris. The instructions they had been given did not leave any doubt that it was she. They left her to conclude her sale to the person who had called her, and bought all that remained, on condition she brought it into a tavern close by. They did not think it appropriate to say anything to her in the open street; but in the tavern into which she followed them, after having asked her her husband's name, where he was and what he did, and she only replying with tears in her eyes, and thus convincing them that they were not mistaken, she finally learnt with inexpressable joy of her husband's fortune and what he had become, and the tenderness with which he still held her. One of the two who had a letter for her, which was not sealed, took it out of his coat-tails as though it were any old piece of paper, and hid the address. But scarcely had she seen the writing than she seized it, exclaiming 'This is his writing!' She was agreeably surprised to find that it was to her that the letter was written.

So many proofs were to be believed. They requested her to send for her children. More tears: only one, a girl, remained to her, her two other children were dead. Her daughter worked gutting cod and in fetching water to remove the salt from it.

In an aside, Challe, who stayed some time in Pondichéry with the Duquesne-Guiton squadron in 1691, adds:

> She [Martin's daughter] was, so I was told, very attractive: I never saw her, being at Hougly with M. Boureau Deslandes, her husband. I saw her mother, who is at Pondichéry with M. Martin, a

woman of around fifty years, who still bears traces of being a very handsome person, and who is none the worse for the filth and dissolution of the Halles among which she had worked so long.

Challe resumes his story thus:

> Those who had found her gave her a thousand francs to fit herself out, both herself and her daughter, so as to present themselves decently to the Company on the first day that it would meet, which they told her. She received there all that she was forced to accept, which she at first refused, for she did not consider herself such a grand lady. Today, there is nothing more of that. She upholds her position very well, and pearls and diamonds cover her with more brilliance that did the scales of the carps she used to sell. Both mother and daughter left on the first available vessel, with a suite of princesses. They arrived happily, not more than five or six years ago. The mother has much intelligence, and in no way employs fishwives' jargon. She is called here simply Madame, or given title of Madame General; and the daughter has married very well and is very happy. (1979, 382–4)

There follows in Challe's book an extremely long section purporting to be the views of François Martin on the French colony, the Dutch, and above all on the untrustworthy nature of the Jesuits (one of them, mentioned by name in Challe's passage, Tachard, was later to give the funeral oration for Martin on his death).

There are few details to add to Challe's account. One is the name of Martin's wife, born Marie Coperly. Her husband must have seen the announcement of the French East Indies Company in the summer of 1664 seeking "French artisans and tradesmen who wished to go and live in the island of Madagascar and throughout the Indies", promising them "the means to gain their livelihoods very honesty with reasonable salaries and inducements". Martin left from Brest on the frigate *Aigle Blanche* at the beginning of March

1665, never to return to France, as the Company's "under-merchant" with the salary of 600 *livres* a year. After short stays in Mascareigne (here Réunion) and Sainte-Marie de Madagascar, he landed at Fort Gaillard on the eastern coast of Madagascar on 26 August. By 1667 Martin had been promoted to "merchant", and was treated by the director-general de Faye with considerable deference.

A word is necessary about the background to the French East Indies Company. Henri IV granted the monopoly of trade between France and the Indies in 1604, following the Dutch and English models, to a group of merchants from Dieppe, Rouen, and St Malo. This came to little, and was reformed in 1642 by Richelieu to service French outposts in Madagascar, but trade with the Indies languished. Colbert made a third attempt to promote this trade, carried on almost entirely in English and Dutch ships, by creating in 1664 the Compagnie des Indes Orientales, which absorbed what remained of the earlier company. Few merchants adhered to it and it was more of a state organization from its inception, most of its capital coming from public entities rather than individual traders. The articles of foundation allowed for a monopoly on navigation and commerce in the Indies, the eastern and southern seas for fifty years; the concession in perpetuity of lands and places occupied, with the right of title; and the concession in perpetuity of Madagascar and the nearby islands on condition of propagating the Christian faith.

The colonization of Madagascar, begun in 1665, was a disaster, and the island was finally abandoned in 1674. A 'factory'—that is, a trading station belonging to a foreign company, sometimes no more than an office, store, or godown—was established at Surat in 1666, and at Masulipatam in 1669 (though by 1671 it was ruined). Pondichéry was set up in 1673. In 1683, on Colbert's death, the Compagnie des Indes Orientales became a state organization;

Colbert's son, the Marquis de Seignelay, Secretary of State for the Navy, was made president and his deputies were all bureaucrats. The trade with the Indies was largely killed after the French minister, the Marquis de Louvois, obtained a prohibition on the import of printed cloth from the Indies.

It was François Caron, formerly in the employ of the VOC, the Dutch East India Company, who was responsible for bringing Martin from Madagascar, which he left on 20 October 1668, first for Cochin, then for Surat, where he and his party arrived on 10 March 1669. After little more than a month, he left on a mission to Bandar Abbas in Persia, not returning to Surat until November, where the French factory was in some disarray and its servants fractious. In May 1670 he moved to Masulipatam, visited Hyderabad, and had a showdown with the Armenian Macara, who, refusing to hand over his accounts, was arrested and sent to Surat. São Tomé de Meliapur, near Madras, was taken by the La Haye squadron in July 1672, and, because trade was declining in Masulipatam, Martin withdrew to São Tomé the following January. Knowing the place lacked victuals which had to be sought from Pondichéry further south on the Coromandel Coast, Muslim forces of the King of Golconda attacked São Tomé. In January 1674, Martin was ordered by de la Haye to Pondichéry, an outpost the general had just acquired. It was flanked by the Danes in Tranquebar and the English in Madras, and by the Dutch, who seized São Tomé from the French in September 1674.

The French Company's Indian base remained at Surat, now under the control of François Baron, but Martin's prestige and position advanced over time. He was summoned by Baron to Surat in 1681, and remained there until 1686. When Baron died in 1683, Martin was elected director-general of the French Company's operations by his colleagues; he was confirmed in this position in January 1686, but he removed to Pondichéry on 20 May the same year.

His re-establishment in Pondichéry at this juncture was extremely important in relation to the activities of the French in Siam. The embassy led by the Chevalier de Chaumont, seconded by the Abbé de Choisy, had been sent to Siam in March 1685, staying there from September to December; the Chevalier de Forbin, the engineer La Mare, and some dozen others had remained in Siam, the first two at the request of the ageing King Narai, doubtless egged on by his wily chief minister Constantine Phaulkon, who had his own Levantine scenario in mind: the establishment of the French in Siam to sustain his own ambition, which some said was the crown itself, but more likely was his continued personal dominance through a pliant ruler.

Mergui, the chief Siamese seaport on the west coast of the peninsula, lay across the Bay of Bengal from Pondichéry, and François Martin was to become increasingly involved in movements to and from the Siamese outpost, which was under French command from the middle of 1687 until after the revolution of May 1688 in Lopburi. This was also a time of considerable turmoil in India, with the fall of the kingdom of Golconda to the Great Mogul, and a declaration of war between Siam and the British East India Company over allegedly unpaid bills run up by Phaulkon on King Narai's behalf.

After the overthrow and murder of Phaulkon, the death of King Narai, and the assumption of the throne by Petracha in July 1688, the French forces in Siam, which had been sent in considerable numbers with the ill-fated La Loubère-Céberet embassy of 1687, were holed up in their fort in Bangkok until November 1688, when they withdrew to Pondichéry led by the incompetent General Desfarges. From that point on François Martin's stance changed from outside observer of Siamese affairs to that of an active, if unwilling, participant. He spoke in vain against the proposed expedition to Junk Ceylon (Phuket) and took part in the military councils held in Pondichéry with the evicted senior French officers.

News slowly filtered through to Pondichéry of the treatment of the French missionaries in Ayutthaya and the remnants of the French forces who fled Mergui. Pondichéry became the temporary base of the Duquesne-Guiton expedition of 1690–91 (in which Robert Challe took part) which was meant to frighten the Siamese and attack Mergui, and in the end did neither. Pondichéry then became the base for the activities of the unloved and meddling Jesuit, Tachard, still determined somehow to return and play a role in Siamese affairs in between running his diamond smuggling operation.

François Martin had a unique viewpoint. He was duty bound to support French activities, but he was a prudent soul and had a businessman's instincts—honed by years of dealings with native princes in India—of what would work and what would not. He tried to establish new trading posts and to this effect sent his son-in-law Deslandes-Boureau to Bengal. He received first-hand accounts of details, supplied by the not disinterested Samuel White, of the massacre of the English in Mergui in 1687. He also had first-hand accounts of the way the French troops conducted themselves in Bangkok, not least over the disgraceful return of Madame Constance Phaulkon to her tormentors in Ayutthaya.

Pondichéry was sold over French heads by Ram Rajah, the Maharatha king, to the Dutch, and finally taken by the Dutch on 7 September 1693. Martin was taken prisoner to Batavia; after his release he went to the trading post at Chandernagor in Bengal. He returned to Pondichéry in 1699, two years after the signing of the Treaty of Ruyswick, and attempted to revive French trade there. To forestall a new attack on the outpost, he built a fort, Fort Louis, which was inaugurated in August 1706. He died four months later, while still director general, on 31 December 1706 at the age of seventy-two. In his funeral oration, Tachard rightly observed that Pondichéry owed everything to him.

The interfering Jesuit Tachard stayed on in Pondichéry after Martin's death, but was soon in conflict with his successor, the Chevalier Hébert, who complained of the priest's authoritarianism and insolence: "You are so used to interfering in the affairs of the Company in spite of the request I made many times to leave us in peace". Tachard finally left Pondichéry ten years later, for Chandernagor (where he died in 1712), not without having put in danger the entire French colony by entering a Hindu temple and demolishing the statues inside. Pondichéry was to remain the chief French outpost in India, notwithstanding being occupied by the British from 1761–3, 1778–83, 1793–1802, and 1803–16. It was finally absorbed into independent India in 1954.

The *Mémoires* of François Martin, begun in 1664, end in February 1694, but effectively terminate with the handing over to the Dutch of the French outpost in September 1693. Written in a very clear unencumbered style, they come to some 1,700 pages, and were written up from notes made throughout his career, with sometimes blanks for dates or details, to be added later. The complete text was published in three volumes by the Société de l'Histoire des Colonies Françaises in Paris, edited by A. Martineau, with introductions by Henri Froidevaux in 1931 (for the years 1665–September 1674), 1932 (October 1674–1688), and 1934 (1689–1694). It is this long out-of-print edition which is the source of the material in this book.

CHAPTER ONE

EARLY FRENCH RELIGIOUS AND COMMERCIAL CONTACTS WITH SIAM

THE first mention in Martin's memoirs of Siam occurs, significantly, in connection with French missionary activity. In November 1672, he wrote from Masulipatam:

> I received letters from Bantam the 21st, from the chiefs of the Company's factory; they informed me that the ship the *Vautour* had arrived safely, that the Right Reverend Bishop of Heliopolis, that great prelate of the Foreign Missions who had embarked at Surat on this vessel to go to Siam, not having found a means of continuing his journey, had decided to go to Bengal and thence to take advantage of the ships leaving for Tenasserim; he did me the honour of writing to me and sent some letters to me for the directors-general. (I, 377–8)

The background to this incidental remark is complex; Martin was to explain it himself much later, in March 1693 (III, 303–4). Pope Alexander VI under the Treaty of Tortesillas of 1494 had accorded to Portugal all missionary work in Asia, but the eclipse of Portugal and the rise of Protestantism in Europe led the French, under 'His Most Christian Majesty' Louis XIV, to support overseas missionary endeavour. The Société des Missions Etrangères de Paris was established in 1659, building on the missionary work of the Jesuit Alexander de Rhodes.

Pope Alexander VII, to avoid Portuguese objections to French Missionaries (missionaries of the Missions Etrangères or Foreign Missions), revived lapsed sees. In 1658 François Pallu was created Bishop of Heliopolis (Baalbeck) and apostolic vicar of Tonkin, Pierre Lambert de la Motte was made titular Bishop of Bérythe (Beirut) with a see stretching from Cambodia to Kiangsi, and Ignace Cotolendi was created Bishop of Metellopolis. Cotolendi died in 1662, to be succeeded by Louis Laneau, who was with Lambert de la Motte already in the mission in Siam. Lambert de la Motte with two Missionaries, Jacques de Bourges and François Deydier, had left Marseilles in November 1660 to go to Siam, arriving in Mergui in April 1662 and reaching the capital Ayutthaya five months later after travelling overland. De Bourges left an account of this in his *Relation du Voyage de Mgr l'Evèque de Béryte, Vicaire Apostolique du Royaume de la Cochinchine, par la Turquie, la Perse, les Indes, etc., jusqu'au Royaume de Siam et autres lieux*, published in 1666, and was astonished at the religious freedom which prevailed: "I do not believe there is a country in the world where there are more religions and where their practice is more permitted than in Siam" (1666: 164). This freedom made Ayutthaya ideal for serving as a base for Missionary endeavour in Indochina. Pallu arrived in Siam in 1664, and returned to Europe in 1665, saw Louis XIV in 1668, and obtained from Pope Clement IX in 1669 an extension of the jurisdiction of the apostolic vicars to Siam. He arrived in Surat in 1671 and went thence to Siam, which he left in 1674.

It is not surprising that Pallu should write to Martin. The layman knew of and admired the work of this 'great prelate' who, he noted on January 1672, had passed through Madagascar the previous year and through the factory of the French East Indies Company in Surat in the same year; though Martin does not say so, Pallu was en route to the mission in Siam.

The next entry for Siam, in March 1675, again concerns Mgr Pallu, Bishop of Heliopolis: "This great prelate, whose probity and sanctity Europe, Asia and America admire, had embarked in Siam on a vessel of a private French merchant to go to Tonkin, to devote the rest of his strength to the conversion of infidels" (II, 13).

The poor bishop and his vessel were detained in Manila, but the mission in Siam had placed 15,000 *livres* in the venture. Pallu was sent to New Spain (Mexico), Madrid, Rome and returned to France. The captain of the ship and the other French were imprisoned in Manila, and finally released after five years on orders from Madrid. After his long voyage from Manila to Europe, Pallu stayed three years in Rome, returning in 1682 to Ayutthaya with presents for the Siamese King Narai from the pope and Louis XIV. He left for China in 1683, to die the following year in Fukien. Lambert de la Motte was to die in Ayutthaya in 1679, and Laneau in 1696.

Buddhist Siam's open policy towards Christian endeavours (in marked contrast to the policies pursued by states in Catholic Europe) can be seen in Martin's third entry relating to Siam, in April 1676, where he notes that on board the vessel seized by the King of Golconda in Masulipatam were "Missionaries of the Missions Etrangères who were there to go to Siam; they were obliged to hide, for fear that in their initial anger the officers and people might arrest them" (II, 44).

Martin had more Missionary news exactly a year later: after giving the latest information received concerning Bishop Pallu, he adds (April 1677):

> I also learnt from letters from Siam that the French Missionaries made many conversions in Tonkin and Cochinchina. Things were not the same in Siam, although this place was like an entrepot for the other missions and from where they were supplied with all essentials. This was attributed to the stupidity of the Siamese, a brutal people to whom one could not explain the mysteries of the Christian religion. (II, 86)

Martin shows no greater prejudice than the other French of the period in respect of those who saw fit not to convert. It should be pointed out that 'Siam' here may mean no more than Ayutthaya, rather than the country as a whole; frequently the same word served, for foreigners, for both.

It is worth observing that Pondichéry was a small outpost at the time, in comparison to the longer established and much bigger British base in Madras. This is confirmed by Martin's comments in May 1677, when he decided to send there, for greater safety, the better part of the goods held in Pondichéry. Madras had more movements in ships too, as is shown in Martin's remarks at the end of 1677 when "Some sailors and soldiers asked my permisson, which I gave, to go to Madras to try and reach Europe in English bottoms" (II, 121).

Ongoing Missionary activity in Siam is recorded in Martin's memoirs. In April 1678 he wrote:

> We also received at the beginning of this month letters from Siam in which we learned that the bishops and the French Missionaries were well received by the king, that Christianity increased notably in the kingdoms of Cochinchina and Tonkin through the zeal and application of these charitable Missionaries. (II, 128)

The following year, in February, Martin's observations confirm that the English were less welcoming of Missionaries:

> The Abbé Sevin, one of the Missionaries in Siam, travelled from that kingdom to this coast [of Cormandel], to continue his journey to France in relation to affairs of the Mission. He expected to embark at Madras on the vessels of the English East India Company, but was refused passage, so he decided to go to Surat to seek necessities for the continuation of his journey. (II, 161)

But relations between the French Missionaries and the Siamese, in spite of the supposed "brutality" of the latter, appeared to flourish. In January 1680 Martin wrote:

> Since the French Missionaries came to Siam, they had so well ingratiated themselves with the king that this prince decided on sending ambassadors to France to offer his friendship to the king and complete freedom in his states for commerce with his subjects. This monarch continued in his resolution. The journey which the *Vautour* was expected to make to Tenasserim was to take these ambassadors on board. The director Mr Baron charged me with writing to the bishops then in Siam to tell them in advance of the despatch of this vessel, so as to inform the king, and for the ambassadors to embark on the ship in Tenasserim. (II, 180)

This is a surprising passage. It is generally held that Narai's desire to send an embassy to France followed the establishment of commercial relations between the two countries by André Deslandes-Boureau, Martin's future son-in-law. But Deslandes did not arrive in Siam until September 1680 (on the *Vautour*). It is thus clear that the despatch of an embassy was in Narai's mind not only long before Phaulkon's arrival to high office in Siam, but also before commercial relations between the two countries were established.

News of Missionary activity continued to be recorded by Martin. In the same month, January 1680, he wrote:

> I received letters from Masulipatam in which I was advised of the death [on 15 June 1679] of the Bishop of Béryte [Lambert de la Motte] in Siam. He was one of the three great men who were the first, following the Rev. Fr Alexandre de Rhodes, the French Jesuit, to undertake to give help to the missions in Tonkin and Cochinchina, which had so much need of succour and which, with their own funds, with the assistance of several pious persons in Paris, gave rise to the establishment of the Foreign Missions which

has produced so much fruit since. Mr de Béryte bore the family name of Lambert; he came from Rouen where he had a position in the Parliament or in the Chambre des Comptes. The second of these great persons was Mr Pallu of Tours, a canon of the cathedral and so well known under the name of the Bishop of Heliopolis. The third, Mr Cotcolandy [Cotolendi] was from Provence, and had a living in Aix-en-Provence and was consecrated with the name of Bishop of Metellopolis...Mr de Béryte died of kidney stones after having suffered long but with admirable and saintly patience.

We learnt by the same letters that there was much persecution of our religion in Tonkin, in Cochinchina likewise. The King of Siam has named ambassadors to go to France, who are expected to carry costly presents; only a vessel to take them was needed. (II, 184–5)

Again this confirms that the first Siamese embassy to France was the result of Missionary influence rather than commercial ties.

In March 1680 Martin returns to the problems of Sieur Duhautménil, the captain of the unfortunate ship which took Bishop Pallu to Manila, and who had been finally released on orders from the King of Spain. "Sieur Duhautménil had embarked in Siam on a private English vessel to go to Surat, and from there to France, hoping that the mission had been reimbursed for the losses he has suffered." (II, 188) But misfortune dogged his footsteps still; his ship sank in the Straits of Malacca after hitting a rock, he managed to reach Malacca, and thence took a Portuguese ship to Porto Novo, a Portuguese outpost near Pondichéry, where he arrived on 25 March, to tell what little he knew of Manila. This gentleman was to make several subsequent appearances in Martin's memoirs.

Early in April 1680 there was a change of plan. Martin received orders from Surat to prepare goods to send to Siam (i.e. Ayutthaya) and Tenasserim, the first lot to go in the *Vautour*, and the second on the *Vierge*, which had been chartered (II, 189). The *Vautour* arrived at Pondichéry on 31 May (II, 193). Deslandes was on board in the capacity of Company merchant. In addition,

> There were on this vessel several Missionaries from the Foreign Missions who were travelling to Siam; they were led by Mr du Chesne, a doctor of the Sorbonne. All these gentlemen were of exemplary piety and probity. Fr Bonnaventure from Parthenay, a Capuchin, had travelled on the vessel to remain at Pondichéry. (II, 193)

The ship also carried 5,000 rupees for Pondichéry, and the partly paralysed Baron enjoined Martin to try to provide a cargo of 12,000 rupees in value for Siam, to increase the amount taken on in Surat. Martin's future son-in-law came with specific instructions:

> Deslandes had orders, after having assessed the situation in Siam, to remain in the kingdom and establish a factory if he judged it advantageous for the Company; otherwise he was to embark with the ambassadors and accompany them to France. He was charged to take the advice in this matter from the gentlemen of the Mission. The captain of the *Vautour*, after taking the ambassadors on board, had to depart thence according to the orders of Sieur Deslandes and go to Bantam, where Sieur Boureau, who had gone there on board the *Soleil d'Orient*, should give orders to have a cargo of pepper ready for France, which should be loaded on the *Vautour* to return immediately thence for Europe. (II, 194)

The *Vierge*, which also arrived in Pondichéry in May (its master cannoneer and a sailor promptly deserted), set sail on 16 June 1680 for Tenasserim (II, 195–6). Mr Louvain, from the Pondichéry establishment, was ordered to take charge of the sale of the cargo, though Martin was apprehensive of poor profits, as he was "well informed that the voyage to Tenasserim would be disadvantageous to the Company". The *Vautour* set sail for Ayutthaya during the night of 16–17 June, with only 6,000 rupees of merchandise taken on in Pondichéry. They had more in store, but these were not in conformity with the samples already supplied, and Martin declined to start the commerce with Ayutthaya by supplying what pleased the sellers rather than the buyers.

On 15 December the *Vierge* returned with poor sales as expected. This was put down to the cargo having been badly arranged in Surat. But Mr Louvain carried news from Tenasserim in the form of letters from Deslandes. The *Vautour*,

> having arrived at the mouth of the river and advice of this having reached the court, the king sent orders to the governor of the fortress of Bangkok to allow passage to this vessel and instructed other officials to give all necessary assistance; however, while waiting for the ship to go upstream, Sieur Deslandes made the first move. He took the letters for the King of Siam, the *barcalon*, prime minister of the kingdom, and others he carried with him. He was lodged in the house of the Mission where the Bishop of Metellopolis and the gentlemen Missionaries received him with particular satisfaction, given their impatience to see an establishment of the Company in the capital of the kingdom of Siam and still more from the help they would receive from the Missionaries who were aboard the *Vautour*.
>
> While in discussion with the *barcalon* about the manner of presenting the letters and presents to the king, Sieur Cornuel, captain of the *Vautour*, was hastening to go upstream with the ship; when he arrived at the fortress of Bangkok, he noticed that the Dutch flag was hoisted there. He had the governor informed that he would not make the salute if the flag was not removed. There was no hesitation in giving him satisfaction, after which this captain fired fifteen cannon shots. These were confusedly returned from the fortress with many more shots than those which came from the ship. The governor then invited the captain to partake of a meal in the fort. He was well received there. The different nationalities

which were in Siam [Ayutthaya] were surprised at this reception, which was out of ordinary.

The visit which Sieur Deslandes had to make to the King of Siam was decided after many difficulties, because the *barcalon* claimed that he ought to make it in the manner of other national representatives, who appeared before the monarch crawling on the ground on their knees and elbows, their heads bowed, which he refused to do. He went to the palace with the customary attendants and had the presents carried there. After entering the audience chamber, he sat on the ground with his legs crossed, following the usual custom in the Indies and, when the king appeared, he inclined his body somewhat. He was very well received, and the presents were found most beautiful. After a few speeches from both parties, the king withdrew, and Sieur Deslandes withdrew as well.

The orders of Sieur Deslandes were to remain in Siam according to the dispositions he might find for establishing a factory in this kingdom or to travel to Europe with the ambassadors, if he did not see occasion to obtain advantages thereby for the Company. After obtaining information about the commerce in those places and not seeing then the likelihood of selling the merchandise in the cargo of the *Vautour*, following the advice of persons with knowledge of the country—and he was enjoined to heed their advice—he decided to stay, while all arrangements were made for the departure of the *Vautour* on which the three ambassadors were to embark, to go to Bantam, take on goods there and continue thereafter their journey to France. Sieur Deslandes was visited after his arrival by the heads of the English and Portuguese [colonies]. The head of the Dutch sent his second-in-command on pretext of asking if he had any goods for sale from those brought in the *Vautour* when this vessel passed by [the Dutch colony of] Malacca, where it hove to a few days. The Dutch *shahbandar* or customs master wanted him to delare the kinds of goods he transported on his ship and their quantity. He was given short shrift; however, as Sieur Deslandes was in a hurry, he replied that he only had gunpowder and cannon balls in his cargo. This nation was not at all happy to see the vessels of the [French] Company take the southern seas route.

As the goods on board the *Vierge* were debited to Siam, Sieur Louvain had orders to follow the instructions of Sieur Deslandes, who wrote to him telling him to leave them in Tenasserim if he could not sell them, and from thence they ought to be able to be transported to Siam [Ayutthaya]. It seems likely that Sieur Deslandes knew, from the cargo in the *Vautour*, of what comprised the cargo of the *Vierge*—goods poorly selected, damaged, and very expensive. He wrote to Sieur Louvain telling him to leave nothing in Tenasserim. (II, 205–7)

Meanwhile, a ship had been hired early in August 1680 and sent to prospect trade in Phuket, here called Jonselon (Joncelang or more commonly Junk Ceylon). It left on 8 September with Sieur Germain as captain and merchant, two other Frenchmen and a local person to serve as interpreter (II, 198–9). The ship returned to Pondichéry on 12 February 1681:

> the voyage had been quite profitable by reason of the tin brought from this island, and which it had formerly supplied in quantity, when it was peopled. Smallpox, which broke out there a few years back and is like the plague on those shores, carried off many of the inhabitants, and the trading which the people of Kedah and Perak formerly carried on had to be abandoned by many. I have a copy of the journal of Sieur Germain about the advantages of an establishment on that island. There were four elephants on board, which the governor [of Phuket] requested me to sell on his behalf. (II, 216–7)

News of the Siamese embassy to go to France reached Martin in Pondichéry in April 1681:

> I received on the 17th letters from Sieur Deslandes written in Siam [Ayutthaya]. He informed me that the *Vautour* set sail on 22

December last, that the three ambassadors had embarked on this vessel, with a suite of twenty valets, fifty or sixty huge packing cases full of presents and a great amount of luggage; that the *barcalon* or prime minister had been informed concerning the quantity of pepper trees in the kingdom which were useless since they were not looked after; people had been appointed to cultivate them and it was hoped that in a few years the kingdom would supply a quantity of this kind of spice. Opinions were also expressed about establishing a Company factory on the Malay coast. (II, 223)

Martin was ever the Company man, and added: "The few goods which had been taken on the *Vautour* in Pondichéry had yielded a good profit, which was not the case of those from Surat, which Sieur Deslandes had trouble in disposing of."

On 5 June 1681 Martin, travelling from Madras to Chicracoly, received further news from Deslandes in Ayutthaya:

Two express messengers from Masulipatam arrived at four in the afternoon; they gave me letters written by Sieur Junet. In the packet there were letters from Sieur Deslandes, describing some particularities of trade in the kingdom of Siam. He also informed me of the news which had been given out of the seizure of the ship from Masulipatam beyond the islands of Tenasserim by the *Vierge*, and said the Moors established in Odia [Ayutthaya], which is the capital, had got together and complained to the *barcalon*, saying that this interrupted all commerce, but this minister did not take them seriously and dismissed them. (II, 231)

Trade with Phuket continued in an intermittant fashion, and news filtered through about the Siamese embassy to France. On 1 October 1681 Martin, then in Surat, noted:

letters came from Sieur Deltor [in Pondichéry], indicating that he was preparing an assortment of goods which he had orders to send to Joncelang. He had received letters from Sieur Louvain in Bantam; the sale of cloth had not been very profitable there, and the *Vautour* was still there as well as the ambassadors of the King of Siam. They were waiting for a vessel which was to be sent from Surat to take them on board and carry them to France. It was thought that the *Vautour* could easily have undertaken the voyage; this delay is at the Company's expense. (II, 273)

The Company's involvement with the Missionaries continued. The Bishop of Heliopolis, the Abbé de Lionne and ten others arrived in Surat from Bombay in October 1681, and concern about the stranded ambassadors in Bantam is shown in Martin's recording, the same month, letters indicating the arrival there in September of the *Soleil d'Orient* and of the embarcation of the Siamese embassy (II, 275), with the *Vautour* returning to Siam. Small-scale trade with Phuket continued from Pondichéry. It was not until January 1682 that some of the Missionaries continued their journey. The Abbé de Lionne and three others were sent overland to Masulipatam, to travel thence by sea to Tenasserim, and then overland to Ayutthaya (II, 285).

The *Vautour* arrived in Surat on 6 March 1682 returning from Bantam and Siam, with letters from Deslandes, who

informed us of the lack of satisfaction he received at that time from the King of Siam and the minister the *barcalon* on the occasions when he went to further the Company's interests; the English and the Dutch, who had been in the kingdom a long time and conducted a great deal of trade, were preferred. (II, 289–290)

This again is interesting, for it is generally assumed that Deslandes had been extremely successful in furthering French commercial interests in Siam right from the beginning, and found the king and his minister of foreign trade easy to deal with; less so than appearances gave out, apparently.

Surat was not the staging post just for French missionaries going to Siam; in April 1682 the Italian Bishop of Argoli, accompanied by two Italian Franciscan missionaries left for Bombay on an English ship to travel from there to Siam. On the 23rd of the same month the Bishop of Heliopolis and the Missionaires set sail for Siam, carrying letters for Deslandes, and from thence to continue to Tonkin (II, 292).

Letters came from Deslandes the following month, confirming

> the little satisfaction he received from the King of Siam and his minister. He believed that recalling him and preparing for his return with a view to completely abandoning the factory would cause the monarch to change his attitude towards the Company. It was thought best to change nothing until after the return of the ambassadors who had embarked on the *Soleil d'Orient* to go to France. (II, 294)

The Company had little luck in Phuket either; in June 1682 Martin received letters from Deltor in Pondichéry indicating that the small ship sent there had returned but the journey had not been profitable (II, 295). However, the Company did not give up hope; Martin noted in September 1682 that letters from Pondichéry indicated another small boat was being prepared to send to Junk Ceylon (II, 302). But the Company was in financial straits; in April 1683 Martin recorded that Pondichéry did not have enough money to buy up sufficient cargo to send to Siam on the *Vautour*, and the ship itself was in need of repairs (II, 316). The ketch *Saint-Joseph* arrived in Surat on 26 April 1683 from Siam and Tonkin, having lost its captain off Cochinchina during an attack by Chinese pirates, and carrying the Missionary Lefèvre "who had served as ambassador to the king of that country and had been well received"; from later remarks it would seem that Lefèvre was received by the ruler of Tonkin. At Ayutthaya "Sieur Deslandes had loaded elephants' teeth [tusks], benzoin, and sappanwood on board" and had embarked

"Mr Lefèvre whom the gentlemen bishops were sending to France for the affairs of their mission"; he arrived in Surat, according to Martin, on 15 May 1683 bringing packets of letters from Siam, at the same time as letters arrived from Ayutthaya via Masulipatam, following the Bishop of Heliopolis's arrival in Ayutthaya.

> Since the visit which he [Pallu] had made to the king, and the letter of our king which he had given this monarch, the court had entirely changed in favour of our nation. The wise conduct of Sieur Deslandes, the head of our factory, had also greatly contributed to this. He had drawn up a treaty with the minister [the *phra klang* or *barcalon*] under which all the pepper cultivated in the kingdom would be delivered to the Company at an agreed price, that it would be free to buy goods directly from the junks which came from China and Japan, and to take goods on board the King of Siam's vessels which it was desired to send thither without paying freight. Sieur Deslandes had procured other advantages for the Company by the same treaty. The return of the ambassadors was awaited with impatience, and as this court was quite sure our king would send with them envoys to tie a close bond of friendship between the two nations, the King of Siam had given orders to prepare and furnish the most important mansion in the city to house them. On the advice which Sieur Deslandes received that the head of the Dutch factory had requested the island of Junk Ceylon, he also sought it from the minister for the [French] Company, in order to spite the Dutch. The result was as he expected: the King of Siam declined to cede this island to one or the other in order not to cause any jealousy. (II, 317–8)

Pallu had first been received by King Narai on 18 October 1673 (Lanier 1883: 15, van der Cruysse 1991: 200–2); he returned to Siam in 1682 on 4 July with presents from the pope and Louis XIV and, for the second time, was received in audience by the king. On the religious front, things proceeded smoothly, as they did on the commercial front, with the able Deslandes in charge of the Ayutthaya factory.

French trading contacts were to increase with Siam, and so was Missionary endeavour; and Deslandes was to establish a good rapport (Martin later hints this might have been too good) with a rising star in Ayutthaya, Constance or Constantine Gherakis, alias Phaulkon.

CHAPTER TWO

TRADE, MISSIONARIES, AND THE EMERGENCE OF PHAULKON, 1683–85

WITH the French factory now established by Deslandes in Ayutthaya, though not without initial difficulties, trade could be expected to flourish, particularly under the impetus of the Siamese embassy sent to France by King Narai, a decision taken before Deslandes arrived in Siam.

But Martin was worried about the lack of news concerning the *Soleil d'Orient*. The ship bearing the Siamese ambassadors to France had sailed from Surat at the end of August 1681 and stopped over at the Ile de France, now Mauritius, to unload some Company goods and take on provisions and water in November. It then set sail for Fort Dauphin in Madagascar (van der Cruysse 1991: 241). Nothing more was heard of it. In January 1684, Martin gloomily noted in his memoirs "As no news had been received of the *[Soleil d']Orient*, it could no longer be doubted that this vessel had sunk without trace." (II, 339) As it was also carrying a considerable cargo of Company goods, the blow was double.

In so far as Siam is concerned, Martin's *Mémoires* at this point have the disadvantage of their optic from Surat, from where, after Baron's death in June 1683, he directed the operations of the French Company. He had lost proximity to Mergui and Ayutthaya.

Nevertheless letters continued to arrive with news of Deslandes' activities and of developments in Siam.

May 1683 finds Martin still trying to develop trade with Junk Ceylon (his 'Joncelang', that is Phuket). The small ketch, the *Saint-Joseph*, is recorded as leaving Pondichéry for a trip to Junk Ceylon and to explore the coast; presumably that near Phuket, since the Coromandel Coast was fully explored. The comings and goings of the Company's several ships are recorded, along with transactions with different Indian states and the other European companies trading in India. Ayutthaya does not figure in Martin's account from Surat until the following February 1684: "We had news on 29th of the arrival at Soualy [the outer port of Surat] of Mr Geffrard, Missionary, and of Sieur Deslandes-Boureau, head of the Company's factory in Siam..." They arrived at the Company's lodge in Surat on 1 March.

Mr Geffrard was sent from Siam with orders to set up an establishment in Surat, with a view to receiving there the Missionaries who would ordinarily pass through there on the Company's ships to go subsequently to join the Right Reverend bishops, and to be sent on into the missions, depending on the need in the fields. The Capuchin friars, established for several years in Surat, feared that carrying out these orders would not be advantageous to themselves or the Missionaries: the Mohammedans, particularly the Mogul [Aurangzeb, r. 1658–1707], did not permit the establishment of priests or religious persons in their states. Perhaps these good fathers had still other reasons; they spoke to us about this and to Mr Geffrard; he had difficulty in giving in to them. However, it was agreed that he would write to Siam and to the Right Reverend bishops. Things remained in this state and were not advanced further...

Sieur Deslandes-Boureau had come to Surat on the orders of the King of Siam. Several reasons had moved this monarch, the first being that he was surprised the Company had not sent any ship to

Siam since the *Vautour* returned from there. He was also pained not to have any news of his ambassadors who had embarked in Bantam on the *Soleil d'Orient* to go to France. This seemed the most important point. The King of Siam was not discouraged about this delay; he knew that sea passages were full of risks and did not always succeed; he did not conceal that his passion was so extreme to enter into friendship with France that, even if an accident had happened to his men, he would send further ambassadors and would not desist until he had contracted this amity with our king. Sieur Deslandes was also charged with obtaining satisfaction from private English merchants who had in their charge personal effects of the King of Siam. Before his departure, Sieur Deslandes had drawn up a treaty of commerce with the king's officials which was very advantageous to the Company. On his advice, pepper trees were being grown in many places around Siam [Ayutthaya]; the Company was to receive the harvest of this pepper at an agreed and very nominal price, the freedom of loading goods on the king's vessels going to Japan without paying freight, the same for the return, and were permitted to sell goods from the factory to such merchants who came, and to buy goods likewise from foreign merchants who might come to Siam from Japan, Manila, China, and other places. This article was a considerable advantage for our commerce in Siam where the king's ministers were often in a position to take for their own account the goods which came from outside, particularly those from China and Japan, which they then sold at profit. There were other articles in the Company's favour which made this treaty extremely advantageous.

Sieur Deslandes had left a merchant and a clerk at the factory in Siam; he had loaded between 10,000 and 12,000 rupees of goods for the Company on the vessel in which he had travelled. (II, 344–5)

So things were going much better for the French in matters of trade, and King Narai had sufficient confidence in Deslandes to use him to effect personal commissions outside his normal fields of duty. Later the same month, Martin wrote:

Sieur Deslandes, having maintained that it was important to send a ship to Siam and to conduct some individual trade to try and keep the king in his positive disposition for our nation while awaiting letters from France, even though money was short, it was agreed to seek means to do so. We bought a ship of 150 tons called the *Saint-Louis* which was prepared for this journey, and orders were given to the broker to obtain goods to constitute a small cargo. (II, 346)

A few days later, Martin added this curious (and commercial) detail:

Everything was got ready for the departure from Surat of the *Saint-Louis*. There was at the lodge a lion of passing size which a Portuguese gentleman had offered as a present; it served no purpose in the lodge and was even a financial burden; it was decided to put it on the *Saint-Louis* and ship it to Siam. (II, 348)

The animal ended up in King Narai's personal menagerie in Lopburi, where French visitors in 1685 noted that it looked like the late Marshal Turenne, perhaps more on account of his style in wigs than in leonine physiognomy (Bouvet 1963: 136). As will be seen below, this recycled gift was apparently appreciated.

Potential trade with the depopulated Phuket was still pursued; the same month Martin wrote that the *Saint-Joseph*, not being needed in Surat, was sent to Pondichéry "to be used for journeys to the island of Joncelang." (II, 348)

The *Saint-Louis* finally left on 12 May 1684:

This vessel had suffered in the roads from bad weather; the Siamese who were to go aboard with some effects for the king their master delayed the departure; however, after having given them all the time to settle their affairs, and the vessel running the risk of being beached, it was despatched. The Siamese had agreed to embark on board a private English trader's ship which was making the same journey, which is what caused them to put off their departure from one day to the next until the *Saint-Louis* set sail. (II, 350)

Martin adds that as no one in the Company's Ayutthaya factory was capable of taking charge of the sale of the cargo, the ship's captain was instructed to call at Pondichéry to take on board Sieur Louvain to oversee this activity. At the beginning of September, he learnt that Louvain carried out his orders, loaded cloth on the *Saint-Louis* and sailed from Pondichéry on 17 June for Siam (II, 360).

Meanwhile Deslandes spoke of his desire to return to France. Martin explained how short-staffed the Company was and Deslandes agreed to stay on. (II, 380)

The next entry touching on Siamese affairs, dated March 1685, is the first in which the new chief minister, the Levantine Phaulkon, is mentioned. It starts off with details of the *Saint-Louis's* success.

> The *Saint-Louis* arrived at the roads on the 7th on its return from the journey to Siam. Sieur Louvain, who had embarked on it at Pondichéry and who was due to return to this post, had taken the route through Tenasserim to get there. He sent his journal to tell us of the state of affairs... They found everything in the Siamese factory as Sieur Deslandes had left it; the goods loaded at Pondichéry had been sold for a reasonable profit, but there was little that could be done with those from Surat.
>
> The lion which we had sent to the King of Siam was well received there; this monarch sent in exchange a present of some Japanese and Manila gold and silverwork worth about 3,000 rupees.
>
> Work was proceeding well on the growing of pepper vines; thirteen thousand men were attending to them and several mandarins were directing them, each man being charged with caring for two hundred plants.

The King of Siam continued to show much affection for our nation. The loss of the ambassadors which he had sent to France and which could no longer be doubted did not discourage him. An envoy from the viceroy of Goa had arrived in Siam [Ayutthaya] with letters of complaint against the Right Reverend French bishops and Missionaries, even containing entreaties that they be required to leave the kingdom, because of the attacks received by the Portuguese priests and religious orders which had been falsely related. The King of Siam, who was better informed, took no heed of this matter. The envoy was not received with distinction which was, he averred, on account of his not having letters from the King of Portugal; the court at Siam nevertheless agreed to send envoys to Goa to return the viceroy's envoy.

Sieur Louvain had some difficulties in Siam concerning the translation of the letters I had written to the *barcalon* where there was question of our king and the King of Siam. The officials of this monarch, as obstinate as the other peoples of Asia about the grandeur of their sovereign, pretended to accord him the rank of emperor and of some rank above a king. It was skilfully shown to them that if it were necessary to distinguish between these terms that it would not be according to their deserts. The problem was solved by placing them on an equal footing.

There was news in Siam [Ayutthaya] of the departure of the bishop of Heliopolis to China...

Mr Constance Phaulkon, from the island of Cephalonia, after divers adventures which are quite well known in France by the published accounts of them, had arrived in Siam and established himself there. He was known to the king who appreciated his wit and raised him to the highest posts in the kingdom; he was then beginning to enter into the affairs of the government. (II, 382–4)

It would seem that Martin at this point added at a later date to his memoirs. Phaulkon was largely unknown in France before the return of the Chaumont-Choisy embassy in the middle of 1686, and it was the published accounts of these gentlemen, and Fr Tachard, which made him well known.

Martin goes on to relate how the *Saint-Louis* was dismasted by lightning just below the bar of Siam on the return journey but managed to reach Surat, where it was put in order to make another journey to Siam, taking on more goods at Pondichéry. He then adds:

> A little time after their departure from Siam, Mr Vacher [Bénigne Vachet] and Mr ... [Antoine Pascot], Missionaries, and two minor Siamese mandarins embarked on an English interloper's ship to go to England. The two mandarins had letters for Mr de Croissy [Secretary of State for Foreign Affairs] to try to obtain some news of the ambassadors who embarked on the *[Soleil d']Orient* and assurances on the part of the King of Siam to send others if these first had not arrived. Mr Vacher was appointed to conduct these two mandarins. (II, 384)

Since it was nearly three years since the *Soleil d'Orient* had left Surat for France, there was indeed every likelihood that the ship had sunk. This was not confirmed until July 1685, when Martin wrote, after noting the report by a French sailor Croisier that all trace of any occupation at Fort Dauphin in Madagascar had disappeared by 1684, the French settlement being in ruins:

> The aforementioned Croisier assured us having learnt at Fort Dauphin that the ship the *Soleil d'Orient* had anchored there, that it was taking on a lot of water, that the natives had told him the names of the captains and the other officers, which were found to be exact, that this vessel, after having negotiated with the people of the island, had set sail and, surprised by a sudden gust of wind, had run aground on the coast at Itapère, and that no one was saved from those on board. As we have had no news of this ship since its departure from Mascareigne [Réunion and Mauritius], there might

be some truth in Croisier's report. The Company was informed. (II, 399)

Itapère is a peninsula to the north of the bay of Fort Dauphin (Tolagnaro), in south Madagascar. Fort Dauphin was founded by the French in 1643, but was abandoned in 1674 after the massacre of the French there (Martin writes about this in II, 28–30).

In April 1685, Martin learnt of the death of the Bishop of Heliopolis in Amoy (II, 389), and the following month noted the passage through Surat of the Missionary Raguienne destined for Siam. There,

> The clerks whom Sieur Deslandes had left on his departure in charge of the factory not being up to supporting the office in a period of [increased] trade I told Sieur Deltor [in Pondichéry] to embark Sieur Louvain on the *Saint-Louis* to go to Siam and to be head of the conduct of the Company's affairs there. Some presents were sent to the King of Siam and the *barcalon* and we wrote to the most important persons in that court. The vessel should also take on board at Pondichéry goods which had been ordered to be held ready to transport there. The Missionary Geffrard had left overland for Masulipatam a few days earlier in order to assume the succession of the late Sieur Junet whom he had left in the mission in Siam. (II, 391)

Things did not go as smoothly as planned though. Louvain had not appeared in Pondichéry from taking the overland route through Tenasserim, and Martin learnt in June 1685 that Deltor was worried on his account (II, 395). However, Louvain finally arrived on 7 June, Martin noted in August, and left on the *Saint-Louis* on 28 June (II, 404).

In August 1685, Martin received a visit from the head of the English East India Company in Surat, with interesting news for the

French: "He told us that from London he had received information that the French Company was expecting to send four ships to the Indies, and that the [French] king was going to send an ambassador to Siam." Martin learnt the ambassador's name, the Chevalier de Chaumont, the following month, from information received from Deltor in Pondichéry who obtained his news from Jewish merchants settled in Madras. The impression that the entire colonies of expatriates in the Orient were writing to each other with whatever straws of news they had is confirmed when Martin adds: "This news was confirmed by a private letter from Paris, which had come on English ships reaching Madras." At the same time, Martin learned that Vachet had arrived at court in Versailles with the two Siamese envoys. He continued with an interesting detail of hurt royal pride:

> The King of Siam is incensed with the Dutch: the monarch claimed that the King of Jambi in the island of Sumatra had not declared the fealty which he ought, and which he had proffered for several years, and stopped when the Dutch Company established itself supreme in the land by building a fortress at Jambi, capital of this small state. The King of Siam had written about this to the king; this monarch excused himself on account of the servitude to which he was reduced by this fortress which left him with only the shadow of his former authority. The King of Siam has complained to the Dutch; they did not pay much heed to his complaints, which irritated him. (II, 405)

Of more importance to the French Company though was the news that "Many pepper vines were ruined in Siam because of floods".

From September more information began to percolate to Surat about the embassy of the Chevalier de Chaumont. Geffrard, the Missionary from Masulipatam, learned through Deltor at Pondichéry that Chaumont would be accompanied by several Missionaries, as well as six Jesuit Fathers who were travelling onwards to China as Louis XIV's mathematicians (II, 406). At the beginning of November Martin learnt from the director of the Dutch Company in Surat that the Chevalier de Chaumont, on the *Oiseau*, accompanied by the frigate *Maligne*, had passed through Batavia and continued the journey to Siam (II, 411); the embassy in fact reached Batavia on 18 August and left on 26 August (Choisy 1993: 119,127). The news took just over two months to reach Martin.

Martin almost never talks about himself in his memoirs, but he records two items of personal importance in December 1685 and the following month. The first entry notes that on 22 April his wife and his second daughter, together with one of the Surat counsellors, Pilavoine, had embarked at Port-Louis on the *Royale* for Surat, but he was extremely concerned at the delay in the arrival of the vessel. The second entry, on 7 January 1686, recorded the arrival in the roads at Soualy of the *Royale*; his wife sent a letter by the ship's longboat. Martin lost no time in going to Soualy, but does not speak of meeting his wife and daughter for the first time in twenty-one years; instead, the good Company man, he opened the Company's packets with M. Pilavoine, who was in them nominated director in Surat and its dependencies, while Martin, "as I had requested", was appointed director of the Coromandel Coast, Bengal, and the southern ports where the Company operated (II, 420).

But the next entry of concern to us is also a personal matter. In February, he wrote; "I had the satisfaction this month of an honorable alliance in marriage between my daughter Marie, who had come to Surat with my wife, and Mr Deslandes" (II, 424). The statement is singularly bald, since there is no likelihood that the two had met before Marie's arrival in Surat the previous month. Deslandes certainly did not let the grass grow under his feet, and clearly marrying the director's daughter would not adversely affect his position in the Company.

CHAPTER THREE

THE FIRST FRENCH EMBASSY TO SIAM,
1685

As seen in the previous chapter, Martin in Surat received indirect news of the decision to send an embassy from Louis XIV to King Narai, of who was to lead it, and who to accompany it. This is not the place to discuss the embassy in detail: the Chevalier de Chaumont, the ambassador, his co-ambassador the Abbé de Choisy, the Jesuit Fr Tachard, another Jesuit Fr Bouvet, and the Chevalier de Forbin all left records detailing its progress. It was meant to impress the Siamese, to obtain the king's conversion, and to obtain favourable terms of trade. On all three counts, except possibly the first, it failed.

Two months before leaving Surat to return to Pondichéry, Martin has an important passage concerning the indifferent success of the embassy. The passage clearly was touched up after the event, for the written accounts to which he refers were not published until 1686 or later, and he would not at this juncture either have seen them or known about them. The hyperbole of the terms employed in respect of Louis XIV was, alas, typical of the time.

> The *Saint-Louis*, returning from a voyage to Siam, arrived on the 19th [March 1686] in the roads of Surat. Sieur Louvain, who had embarked at Pondichéry for this journey, came on shore the same day. Subjects for discussion were not lacking concerning the

36

embassy of the Chevalier de Chaumont who had been sent on our king's behalf. There are so many printed accounts of this voyage by persons of distinction who were party to secrets and details of the embassy that it does not behove me to expatiate on what I know about it. It is certain that the basis for sending of the Chevalier de Chaumont was the assurance that had been given to His Majesty that the King of Siam was of a disposition to embrace the Christian religion. That great monarch, zealous for the conversion of infidels and heretics, seized every occasion for the salvation of these idolaters and lost sheep; every corner of the known world is filled with the proofs of this great zeal. The ambassador did not find in the King of Siam this disposition which had been hopefully proclaimed; he was well received, well treated and so on. Mr Constance Phaulkon, having reached by the king's inclination and his own intelligence the most important posts in the kingdom, took care to accord us all honours; it is said that the Chevalier de Chaumont was nonetheless not satisfied in respect of his conduct of the negotiations on the articles he had to determine for the establishment of our nation in the kingdom of Siam, and it is certain too that, in regard to commerce, the treaty which Sieur Deslandes had concluded was much more advantageous than that which the ambassador obtained. However, the King of Siam, proud of this embassy and full of admiration of the great qualities of our king, named three officials at his court to go as ambassadors to France with the Chevalier de Chaumont. The Rev. Fr Tachard, head of the Jesuits who were destined to go to China, decided to return with the Siamese; he left orders to the other priests to continue their journey according to His Majesty's intentions. The Siamese ambassadors were loaded with very rich presents for the king, for Monseigneur [the king's son], for Mme the Dauphine, for all the royal house and all the ministers. We shall see subsequently in this account the success of this embassy. (II, 425–6)

There is one major error of fact here. Tachard was not the head of the party of six Jesuits destined to go to China, though he certainly acted as though he were. Their head was Fr de Fontaney, who eventually arrived in China after many vicissitudes in 1688.

Martin continues:

Sieur Véret had been sent from France by the Company to become head of the factory in Siam since it was learnt in France that Sieur Deslandes was in Surat. Sieur Louvain, who had embarked at Pondichéry to occupy this post, did not hesitate to cede to the orders of the directors-general; he re-embarked on the *Saint-Louis* to go to Surat. Mr Constance Phaulkon was furthermore not satisfied with his conduct; he complained about him in letters which he wrote to us; since his rise to power, he had become extremely jealous of his position, his character was somewhat violent, and he did not suffer to be contradicted. Sieur Louvain spoke to him rather brusquely about the delays in freeing goods from the King of Siam's stores; he was concerned about the quickening monsoon. Mr Phaulkon thought this liberty showed a lack of respect and he had to be made an example of in Surat in order to obtain satisfaction.

The loss which had been sustained the previous year to the pepper vines by the flooding of the river had been repaired. Others had been planted on the heights above the flood levels and had taken root.

The Abbé de Choisy, who had gone to Siam with the Chevalier de Chaumont, had orders from the king to stay there as His Majesty's resident if the King of Siam embraced Christianity and if he saw in him a disposition to appreciate our religion. As there seemed no likelihood of this, he had embarked to return to France. The Abbé de Lionne had also embarked on the same voyage at the request of the King of Siam to conduct the ambassadors and assist them in behaving according to our customs. All the nations in Siam came in great number to pay their respects to the Chevalier de Chaumont; only the Portuguese were lacking. The Dutch

Company was much alarmed at this embassy; it is jealous of the establishment of the French in the southern seas.

The *Saint-Louis* arrived loaded with all kinds of merchandise; it was unloaded and then entered the river to be refitted. Sieur Véret sent nothing to France in return for the capital which he had been advanced; he excused himself to the Company on account of having found no goods to buy; he sent us a polite letter. (II, 426–7)

Already, Phaulkon's overweening pride can be discerned, and so can Véret's incompetence: he had no idea how to function to the advantage of the Company.

Martin then returns to more humdrum matters for a while. The *Vautour* after repairs was sent to Mergui to wait there for the goods which the *Saint-Joseph* was to bring from Bengal. But Phaulkon's rise to power caused ripples in the Bay of Bengal beyond the extent of Siam there. In April 1686, Martin wrote:

The King of Siam having been unable to obtain satisfaction from the King of Golconda over some trouble which had arisen involving his commercial agent at Masulipatam, he resolved (and it is said on the counsel of Mr Constance Phaulkon) to obtain it himself. This monarch ordered the governor of Mergui to arm two small vessels and to send them to patrol the coasts of Golconda. One private captain, named Sieur Coche, was in charge of this enterprise; he took with him sixty Europeans from divers nations and came to drop anchor before Masulipatam. As nothing untoward was anticipated, he went ashore as night fell with the best of his men and seized the customs house; they pillaged what they could take away, and set fire to it and some nearby houses before withdrawing. A longer stay would have been dangerous for them. But the fire spread even though breaks were established, and the whole town was threatened with being engulfed. The people in the Dutch factory behaved best and were the most concerned by the proximity of their lodge to the houses on fire. The King of Siam's vessels set sail; the people on board made other raids in different places on the coast before withdrawing afterwards to Mergui. (II, 432–3)

Martin left Surat on 29 April and went by boat, via Goa, to Pondichéry, where he arrived on 20 May 1686, and where he was to remain for many long years. Deslandes and "his family" (i.e. Martin's daughter) formed part of the group making the journey. Though Martin found the lodge in almost the same condition he had left it, there was much disunity among its personnel. In spite of all the letters he had to write and transmit, he prepared a cargo of goods to send to Siam on the *Saint-Louis* (II, 439). Mr Louvain had received letters from Siam:

> It was confirmed that the Chevalier de Chaumont had left much displeased with the conduct of Mr Constance Phaulkon. He had arrived in Siam with the Chevalier de Forbin, a lieutenant in the navy. The king had asked Mr de Chaumont to put him at the head of the Siamese troops. This gentleman is a scion of the best families in Provence. Also remaining in Siam is Sieur La Mare, engineer, to see to the fortifications of the stronghold of Bangkok. (II, 441)

Forbin had had to have his arm twisted before he agreed to staying (Chaumont had to give him a formal order, confirmed in writing, to remain); we do not know what La Mare's sentiments were. As Forbin makes no mention of La Mare in his account of his stay in Siam, even though they were probably in Bangkok at the same time, it would seem that the two did not see eye to eye.

The Chaumont-Choisy embassy indeed achieved little: no conversion of King Narai (or anyone else), a worse trade treaty than was already in existence, and a treaty concerning the rights of Catholics which Phaulkon never dared make public. It did, though, carry some three hundred bales of presents for the court at Versailles, and the three Siamese ambassadors, headed by Kosa Pan (Ok-phra Wisut Sunthorn), who was to become *phra klang (barcalon)* in 1688. As Martin noted, the embassy returned with Fr Tachard; he carried secret letters and instructions from Phaulkon, and a licence to operate independently of, and unknown to, the Siamese envoys.

Missionary activity meanwhile continued in Siam, and Pondichéry remained a staging post. In July 1686 Martin noted the passage of the Abbé Pallu "one of the directors of the seminary of the Foreign Missions in Paris", accompanied by a Missionary. Pallu, a brother of the late Bishop of Heliopolis, was due to continue his journey to Siam for the mission, and left in September on the *Coche* (II, 444, 449). This Company ship, to avoid bad weather in the roads of Pondichéry from October to December, was to take shelter in Mergui. As elsewhere in his memoirs, Martin noted the varying alliances and wars of the Indian rulers, and the temporary seizure by the Dutch of Masulipatam from the ruler of Golconda.

The kingdom of Siam, though, was then shaken by two major upheavals, and the Chevalier de Forbin quit the country between the two.

CHAPTER FOUR

THE MAKASSAR REVOLT OF 1686
AND SIAMESE PROBLEMS WITH MADRAS

AFTER the departure for Siam of the *Coche* with the Abbé Pallu on board in September 1686, Martin was apparently without news of the country until 2 January the following year, when the *Saint-Louis* dropped anchor at Pondichéry (II, 455). The captain disembarked, and so, to Martin's possible surprise, did the Chevalier de Forbin, who was supposed to be commanding the King of Siam's forces.

The packets which were handed to us and verbal accounts informed us of the state of affairs in Siam. I have already noted in this memoir that the Chevalier de Forbin had remained in Siam on the request of the king to the Chevalier de Chaumont. That officer had applied himself with much success to the Siamese language and in training the troops of that nation under his command, so that they conducted their drill with as much precision as troops trained in Europe. His deportment and his wise conduct had attracted the king's esteem and the friendship of several mandarins. It is not known if this reputation did not give cause to the rise of Mr Constance Phaulkon's jealousy. It happened at this time that a body of Makassars, who were established in Siam [Ayutthaya] and had their quarter there, conspired in a plot, according to what was said, to kill the king and put in his place one of his brothers or a prince of their nation who had escaped with them from Makassar where he ran the risk of losing his life following revolutions which had occurred in those islands. The plot was discovered before it could take place; Mr Constance, who was then in a strong position, took on the task of destroying this group. He assembled Siamese and native Christians [of Portuguese descent], joined by twelve or fifteen Frenchmen as well as some English under Captain... [there were two: Udall and Coates]; this body of men advanced over the water to the Makassar quarter. These persons, who numbered at most two hundred, warned of the attack on them, were prepared for it. Not every precaution was taken after going on shore before attacking them, the attackers threw themselves on them without taking account of order or rank; the Makassars, with typical determination and resolution, swooped down on this body of men and sent them off in rout, with Mr Constance running the risk of losing his life and being obliged to withdraw. Four Frenchmen were killed: Sieur de Rouen, a private merchant who had been in Siam two or three years; a Company clerk; and two others. The English captain [both Udall and Coates died] fell fully armed into the river where he drowned; two other Englishmen died there. The Makassars foresaw at once that the attack would be renewed and that no quarter would be given; it is said that some killed their mothers and their children while awaiting the second attack.

Mr Constance, having escaped this predicament, took better precautions. They returned to the attack, the prince was killed there, two of his sons were made prisoner, the elder of whom, fourteen years old, only gave himself up after seeing his father lifeless and his body covered with wounds. Some Makassars were killed, others escaped into the woods and were given chase. Some perished there, their arms in their hands. Some were taken and then executed. Fifty took to a boat to save themselves. It had to pass before the fortress of Bangkok where the Chevalier de Forbin was in command as governor. Mr Constance wrote to him to arrest the plotters and try to take them by deceit to spare bloodshed. This gentleman took his precautions and got his men ready. The boat appeared, and dropped anchor in front of the fort. The Makassars went ashore and three or four of the leaders went to parley with the

Chevalier de Forbin who was in a room. A row of pikemen formed a kind of barrier and musketeers were behind them, all Siamese or native Christians. The Makassars, noticing this arrangement, knew nothing could save them. Those who were in front, their kris in their hands, swooped down with surprising intrepidity on the pikemen and musketeers, who abandoned post. The Chevalier de Forbin seized his pistol hard by and wounded the leader. Some Europeans who were also taking part in the events likewise attacked. The men were then reassembled and set fire to all the persons who had taken refuge in the huts and who despatched those found there. Some were killed, others fled to the woods where they were subsequently killed or arrested and punished with divers kinds of death.(II, 455–7)

Martin undoubtedly obtained this graphic account from Forbin, but it is not entirely accurate, as Forbin's own memoirs and other documents show. The Makassars had installed themselves in Ayutthaya, with the consent of King Narai, as a consequence of the Dutch occupation of their homeland. Their revolt there took place in two stages; in the first, in July 1686, the attack on their quarter was unsuccessful, and it was then that Phaulkon, to reduce the number of opponents on hand, allowed fifty-three to leave in a boat with a laissez-passer which he contradicted in his letters to Forbin. At Bangkok, Forbin was instructed to block the passage of the boat and capture the Makassars, but he little knew the damage a kris could cause in the hands of a determined opponent. He lost 356 men in the first day of the skirmish. The second attack on the Makassar camp in Ayutthaya occurred in September 1686, and this time was successful: Phaulkon had placed spiked stakes in the river's waters which the Makassars did not see as they rushed to attack the Siamese forces, though it was on this occasion that a number of Europeans were killed. The two young sons of the Makassar prince were taken to France, baptised in Versailles in 1688, and put in the navy. The elder stabbed himself to death, and the younger was devoid of all humanity, according to Deslandes' son, André-François

Deslandes-Boureau, who saw him in Brest years later (van der Cruysse 1991: 417–8).

Forbin's tale to Martin was perhaps thin on his reasons for leaving Siam. In his memoirs, Forbin claimed that Phaulkon was jealous of his credit with the king (something earlier hinted at by Martin, probably cued by Forbin himself), and that the chief minister had tried to poison him. When he failed to do this, he gave him Herculean tasks to perform, such as arresting the unassailable Makassars or seizing Captain Lake on a well-defended English ship in the roads out of Paknam. To get even with Phaulkon in the latter instance, he took with him a relative of Phaulkon's wife in a potentially dangerous plan to take Captain Lake off his ship by deceit. This action by the French governor of Bangkok was not appreciated by the Levantine chief minister in Ayutthaya, nor his part-Japanese, part-Portuguese, part-Bengali wife, as can be seen.

In the accounts received from Siam, there were native Christians who were relatives of Madame Constance, who wrote disparaging the conduct of Mr de Forbin. Mr Constance who was already opposed to him either though jealousy, as I have already observed, or pressed still more by his wife, who thought that her relatives in Bangkok should not have been treated thus, wrote to the Chevalier de Forbin in rather strong terms, for not having sufficiently taken due caution. This gentleman, naturally hot-tempered, could not bear to be treated in kind; furthermore there were some expressions in the letter which damaged his reputation had he not been well known, and he sent a rather proud reply back. There was, though, a kind of reconciliation, but as the two were not disposed to renew their initial understanding, they subsequently broke off relations over subjects which were not worth while and about which one would have given no thought at other times. The Chevalier de Forbin decided to withdraw on his own account and his friends thought he was rather too quick in this action. Letters were written on both sides; finally, this gentleman, adhering to his plan, was sent an order from the King of Siam in the form of banishment and to withdraw within three days from his command. It was seen as Mr Constance's resentment, but he pushed things too far. The Chevalier de Forbin, not having ready means to carry out this command, withdrew to the *Saint-Louis* which stayed for a few days in the river and then came to Pondichéry.

The captain of the *Saint-Louis*, according to his initial orders, was to travel from Siam to Surat without landing anywhere. Véret, the head of the factory in Siam, advised us that he had engaged the captain to drop anchor at Pondichéry to give us letters he had written to the Marquis de Seignelay [the Secretary of State for the Navy] and the Company. These were of extreme importance and he did not think it fit to send them through Mergui to be put on board the *Coche* for fear of their being intercepted en route. These letters were addressed to me with a partial seal so that I could read them. They dealt almost exclusively with the conduct of Mr Constance. Sieur Véret described him in outrageous terms; his passion was too evident and it was easy to see that the letters would not be well received in France. It was also proposed that the Company undertake various activities in which those who knew the situation did not see much chance of success. This error was common in many persons who were new to the Indies, even among people of distinction; it comes from giving credence to reports without examining the character of those who supply them. In respect of Mr Constance, the high office which he had reached had made him extremely proud, and accustomed to dealing with the Siamese, a grovelling people, cowardly and perfidous, only to be subdued by harsh treatment, the rack, and revolting tortures. He seemed intent on putting the Europeans on the same level: he had very badly treated Sieur de Rouen, a private merchant who was killed in the first attack on the Makassars, and as he was all-powerful, he had Sieur de Rouen seized and sent to Bangkok with an order for him to be put in the stocks where he remained for three months, and condemned him on his own authority to a fine of one thousand *livres* which he had to pay. (II, 457–8)

Martin's language is unusually circumspect in the first paragraph quoted above; he is clearly trying to accommodate both sides, Forbin and Phaulkon. The details given by Martin in respect of de Rouen do not correspond exactly to those found in Forbin's memoirs. The trouble arose with de Rouen because Phaulkon wished to acquire cheaply his supply of sandalwood; he had de Rouen put in the stocks in Ayutthaya, not Bangkok, and Véret complained to the king, who was angry with Phaulkon. Forbin saved Phaulkon's skin by saying, without truth, that de Rouen had been expelled from France for being a Protestant (news of the revocation of the Edict of Nantes could not yet have reached Ayutthaya), and that Phaulkon was always supportive of the French. Martin resumes:

> Even Mr Constance's enemies conceded that he was a very clever person, of broad intelligence, capable of great things, determined and generous, but his ambition, his intolerable vanity which went as far as requiring everything to submit to him, greatly tarnished all these fine qualities which would have distinguished him without the detractions that he supplied. I only received a brief note from him by the *Saint-Louis*; he would write fully via the *Coche*. (II, 458–9)

This summary of Phaulkon's character is virtually the same as that which appeared in Forbin's memoirs, not published until 1729 in French, long after Martin's death:

> Mr Constance had a Soul that was great, noble, and sublime, and such a superior Genius as enabled him to conduct the greatest Projects to in Issue, with a world of Prudence and Sagacity. Happy Constance! if all these great Qualities had not been clouded over by gross Defects, especially by a boundless Ambition, by insatiable Avarice, often even to a Degree of Sordidness, and by a Jealousy, which, taking Fire on the least Occasion, render'd him harsh, cruel, implacable, insincere, and capable of the most hateful Things in Life. (Forbin 1731, English ed: I, 243–4)

Clearly Martin was influenced by Forbin's judgment; Forbin was on the spot in Pondichéry to give his version of events. But Martin had access to other reports, though those of Véret he obviously distrusted, as can be seen in Martin's judgment of Véret's letters to Paris. The French cause was not helped by Véret, a Parisian jeweller with no experience of the East, being almost from the beginning on extremely bad terms with Phaulkon. To make matters worse, Martin noted that the Surat goods sent to Siam could not be sold, and the remaining cargo on the *Saint-Louis* belonged to the King of Siam.

The *Coche* finally arrived in Pondichéry on 4 January 1687, having taken on at Mergui a cargo of sappanwood and some rice, the Company's goods having been sent overland to Véret in Ayutthaya. The ship brought the expected letters from Phaulkon:

> We received letters from Mr Constance; they were filled with complaints about the conduct of the Chevalier de Forbin. He sent copies of letters which this gentleman had written him as well as the replies he had made in which he intended to condemn him. He appeared extremely incensed by him. Mr Constance sent goods on the *Coche* on his own account, and by the same means other letters in which he informed us of his intentions. The two sons of the Makassar prince killed in Siam [Ayutthaya] in the uprising were on board the *Coche*. Mr Constance wrote that they should be sent to France; it was feared that by leaving them in Siam they might become over time leaders of a group to avenge the death of their father. (II, 460)

The French had nothing to do with the Makassar community in Ayutthaya, but Phaulkon was clearly using his influence with the French to get rid of unwanted persons in Siam. What was offered in return for these exiles, if anything, is not known—possibly no more than the chance to make distinguished conversions.

Franco-Siamese trade then received a further setback which was not the fault of Véret or Forbin, namely the threat of war between Siam and the English Company.

Two vessels anchored the 12th [January 1687] in the roads of Pondichéry, the larger flying the red ensign, the smaller one white. The larger fired twenty-one rounds of cannon shot; the pilot then came ashore and gave us a packet from Mr Constance, and letters from Messrs Barnabé and With [Burnaby and Samuel White], both English, the first governor of Mergui, and the other *shahbandar* or customs master. We learned from these that the larger ship belonged to the King of Siam; there were on board some presents which this monarch or Mr Constance were sending to France, and several bales from the same as well as cases of tea on his account; he indicated to me in the letters he wrote that if there were two Company ships in Pondichéry going to France, to divide these goods between them, but if there were only the *Coche*, to put half on board and to put the remaining half in store until another year. I was charged on his part with making three proposals to the Company: (1) if it thought fit, that he enter into its corporate body using the proceeds of the sale of his goods; (2) if it did not agree to this, to take the amount due at the prevailing rate of interest, and, if it refused both these proposals, (3) to hold for him what was due until he had taken his dispositions according to the replies he received. He requested me and Mr Deslandes together to sell these goods as well as the ship which we learnt was a prize taken from Armenian merchants established in Madras. For some time the English Company in Madras and Mr Constance were in dispute, though they were close friends previously, and if one may be allowed to say so, the personal interest that each had was more the cause of this rupture than the reputation and the interests of their masters.

Mr Constance had brought the King of Siam to make as good as a declaration of war against the English, and the seizure of the ship which was sent to us loaded with alum and sappanwood was a consequence of this. We were also well informed that the governor of Madras was seeking an excuse for reprisals. (II, 461–2)

All this placed Martin in a predicament: the governor of Madras would soon learn of the arrival of the Siamese ships at Pondichéry, and while the *Coche* was capable of opposing any English action, it would cause a breach with the English which "did not suit the Company's interests". Finally, "we resolved to refuse absolutely to receive the ship loaded with sappanwood and alum." (II, 462) The captain of the Siamese ship announced that his orders were "to escort this ship to Pondichéry and to hand it over to us, and he abandoned it to us" (another example of Phaulkon's cavalier attitude). The confrontation continued, until the captain of the Siamese ship received news that Madras had indeed sent two ships to search for and attack wherever they found the Siamese vessels. The captain set sail at once. Three days later, on 17 January, the English vessels arrived seeking the Siamese ships. They were informed they had left already. Equal rounds of cannon shot were agreed to, and the English departed, honour having been satisfied (II, 463).

This little incident shows just how high-handed Phaulkon had become; he felt he could dictate his terms to the French Company and treat its employees as his lackeys. It also shows that Phaulkon was trading to a considerable extent on his own account, probably just using the name of the King of Siam, and was seizing prizes like any common pirate in the name of the Siamese king.

Relations were patched up between Siam and Golconda though. Martin wrote in February 1687:

> The King of Siam having interest in maintaining relations with the King of Golconda for the commerce driven between Mergui and Masulipatam, sent an ambassador there with some presents.

They were well received and harmonious relations were re-established. (II, 467)

A small ship came from Mergui the same month bearing letters indicating that the affair of the two ships sent off the previous month caused problems there. While it was in the Pondichéry roads, an English vessel came and cut its cable, taking it off as a prize to Congimer. Martin was embarrassed, but had neither ships nor men to object. Instead, he wrote to the governor in Madras, who replied he knew nothing about it, and would reply when he had further details. He added that he had orders from England to make war on the King of Siam and that effects belonging to him should not be loaded on board ship. "We replied as appropriate, but the small ship remained in the hands of the English; its cargo included sixty chests of copper belonging to an official in Mergui." (II, 468–9)

The same large Siamese vessel which had come to Pondichéry in January reappeared in March. The captain had hidden with his cargo among the islands off Mergui and returned to learn how things stood with the English in Madras. While Martin and he were conferrring, news was given that a large vessel in full sail was approaching from the south. The captain went on board his ship in haste: the approaching vessel carried the English flag. The Siamese ship cut its mooring ropes and sped off, chased by the English vessel (II, 472).

Another large Siamese vessel appeared on 3 April, bearing letters from officials in Mergui and carrying a cargo of 20,000 écus of alum and the metal tutenag. The captain was warned of the risk he ran: there was known to be an English warship to the south which could arrive in a few hours. The captain decided to withdraw.

Two more ships came on the 10th; one of them carried its flag at half-mast and fired a cannon shot. Mr Charmot, of the Siamese mission, was brought ashore. He had boarded at Ayutthaya a vessel of the English East India Company.

> He had been made to undertake the voyage by Mr Constance; he carried packets and presents for the court of England. It was thought he made this move to complain of the conduct of officials of the Company, who had obliged the King of Siam to break with them and declare war on them. Others were more of the opinion that Mr Constance was seeking the protection of a powerful nation; he was making advances to humour England in case France did not reply to his intentions. The ship had suffered since its departure from Siam; several people had died of illness... (II, 474–5)

Charmot decided to continue his journey overland taking a few presents and packets, the rest to go with another person of the cloth on the boat. Charmot, as will be seen, did not carry out this resolution. "There was no special news from Siam. Mr Constance was ever more in favour with the king and dealt with matters with the authority of a prime minister." News came of a big Dutch vessel, with 1,100 men on board destined for Siam, which sank in the Strait of Banka. The men were saved. "It was suspected that some design was formed on the Kingdom of Siam. The Dutch Company was jealous of the understanding which was forming between the French and the Siamese, and of the sending of reciprocal embassies." (II, 474)

Letters from France came in April 1687 to Martin in Pondichéry informing him that two large and two small ships were to arrive to drive a good trade with Siam. But news was still lacking of the return to France of the Chevalier de Chaumont, who in fact reached Brest with the Siamese ambassadors to Louis XIV on 18 June the previous year. In was not until May 1687 that Martin received confirmation of Chaumont's arrival and the understanding the "enterprise" in Siam would be pursued with vigour (II, 480). The elder brother of the late Sieur de Rouen, who was killed in the Makassar revolt, arrived in Pondichéry the same month to travel on the *Saint-Louis* to look into his brother's affairs in Siam (II, 481).

He was not alone in his desire to go aboard this ship. The Chevalier de Forbin, in May 1687, also wished to travel to Siam on it.

He used many reasons to persuade us that it was absolutely necessary that he undertook the voyage. The state in which he had left things on his departure was drawn to his attention: Mr Constance was extremely displeased with him, this kind of banishment which he had received signified that he was unlikely to be well received, as things stood the same; furthermore his passage on the *Saint-Louis* could cause prejudice to the Company's officers. Mr de Forbin did not give in one jot to these reasons; his fiery temperament made him hold fast. We were even obliged to tell him that he would definitely not be permitted to embark on the ship. Our decision caused him to present us with a petition in which he discoursed on the reasons which required him to seek to undertake this voyage, even that he was going in our king's name; he then made protestations to persuade us of the difficulties which would arise if his voyage was opposed. The reply to his petition and the final conclusion was an absolute refusal for him to embark. Things remained thus. We learned later that on the advice he had received that two vessels were being prepared in Madras to be sent to Mergui, rumoured to wage war on the King of Siam (but, according to apparently more reliable opinions, to carry complaints in letters which the governor of Madras wrote to this monarch about Mr Constance's conduct in respect of the English Company), he had written to friends in Madras to try and obtain permission to travel in one of these vessels. It was not likely to have been granted, but as he only decided rather late to take this route, the vessels had already set sail when these letters were received. (II, 482)

Forbin in his memoirs makes no mention of his evident desire to return to Siam, and indeed says he was glad to have left the country at the end of 1686 when he travelled on the *Saint-Louis* to Pondichéry. The reason for his desire to return is as hard to fathom today as it was to Martin in May 1687; one can only speculate that he wished to continue his private trading (the list of goods Forbin cleared through the French customs on his return to France is impressive). But that, given Phaulkon's displeasure with Forbin, would have been extremely difficult.

The *Saint-Louis* finally set sail for Siam on 1 July 1687. Martin appears to defend Forbin in his correspondence with Phaulkon.

> In the letters we wrote to Mr Constance we felt obliged to dwell on the subject concerning the poor treatment to which Frenchmen had been exposed by his orders, which had never been sanctioned before by him in respect of any other European, and it was to degrade nations in this way. Apart from our belief that he would have special consideration for our nation, we considered this matter a serious one; all this in such terms and with all possible civility. (II, 485)

Forbin finally left on 22 August on the *Président*, together with Deslandes, bound for Mergui via Masulipatam (where Forbin gives in his memoirs a graphic account of the city visited by the plague, from which he and Deslandes narrowly escaped).

But the Makassar revolt of 1686 was a signal that, in spite of surface calm, all was not well in the state of Siam. The Mergui massacre the following year confirmed this.

CHAPTER FIVE

THE MASSACRE AT MERGUI, 1687

SIAM began to take on increasing importance as far as the French in Pondichéry were concerned. In July 1687, Martin, apparently ill at the time, noted the passage of two English ships in search of a vessel belonging to Mr Samuel White, the customs master of Mergui, who was proposing to send some 30,000 or 40,000 *écus* in silver to the French factory, to be placed in local trade goods. White (for Martin "Sieur With") was little more than a semi-licenced pirate operating in the Bay of Bengal, and the East India Company was determined to put an end to his operations (II, 486–7).

Missionaries continued to use Pondichéry as a stop-over point to and from Siam; in August 1687 Martin recorded the presence of a "Mr Gravé, a priest from the mission in Siam" who wished to go to Masulipatam where the church had been burnt down in a fire and the Portuguese priest had died in penury. But Masulipatam was in a bad way; letters arrived from Deslandes on 1 October indicating that the plague had left only 300 persons alive in the city, and they were dying. He had left the stricken city on 3 September to continue his journey to Mergui (II, 498).

But Missionaries were not always blessed with good fortune. Charmot, a Missionary from Siam (already mentioned as arriving in April 1687 in the previous chapter), is recorded in October 1687 as having passed through Madras to take an English boat to Europe, but on setting sail the ship had sunk in a violent storm. Martin had opposed Charmot taking the ship, thinking it better to wait for one of the French Company's vessels. Some wreckage was washed up on shore, including a chest belonging to Mr Charmot, with letters for the King of England, for the English East India Company, and some for France. The English in Madras took these documents to the fort there. Letters were discovered from Phaulkon to the directors of the EIC in London complaining of the conduct of the governor and other officers in Madras. They comprised "a string of accusations and invectives against them, accusing them of the disorders which had occurred in the Company in the Indies and which had forced the King of Siam to declare war on them." Some persons in the Madras Council were for arresting Charmot. Charmot learnt that his papers had been found and requested them; the English denied obtaining possession of the papers (even though one Mr Gray in the Council admitted having seen them and handed them over), and Charmot returned once more to Pondichéry, his tail between his legs (II, 501–2).

Poor Charmot did not apparently exert a good influence on the elements. In January 1688, Martin wrote that the English ship in which the Missionary had travelled from Siam to Aceh, wanting to go from there to "Bancoul" (Bencoolen), had gone aground and been smashed to pieces. "Mr Constance was involved for more than 50,000 *écus* in presents and goods in this loss." (II, 507)

The first news of the massacre of the English in Mergui on 25-26 July 1687 apparently only reached Pondichéry in December, and then via a Company employee in Aceh in Sumatra writing on 9 October. "Sieur With", Samuel White, the *shahbandar* at Mergui, had arrived in Aceh having "happily escaped there the massacre which was perpetrated on the English who lived there or were in the King of Siam's service." Martin notes he would have further occasion to speak with more knowledge on the subject (II, 505-6).

That occasion arrived in January 1688, when on the 14th a ship flying the English colours anchored off Pondichéry, and the following day White, the former customs collector of Mergui, came ashore, and related "the disorders of Mergui". What follows is important, being White's version of events, in which he was heavily implicated.

An English ship had arrived in this port [of Mergui] with letters from the governor and the council of Madras to the King of Siam, in which satisfaction was sought of this monarch for the affronts offered by his subjects or on his orders to the English nation. A time limit of sixty days was given in these letters for a [satisfactory] reply, which, if not forthcoming, the captain of the English vessel had orders to declare war and carry out all acts of hostility as occasion presented. The letters were sent express to Siam [Ayutthaya]. Mr White, a fortnight later, went up to Tenasserim on business. During his absence the English captain seized a ship belonging to the King of Siam which was in port, and another belonging to Mr White; he put his own men on board, and made them anchor four leagues below the point where he had anchored since his arrival in Mergui. The Siamese had blocked the approach with a line of stakes in the belief that this would prevent entrance to and egress from the port. This was breached and the Siamese who opposed this action suffered severely. On receiving news of this attack, Mr White returned to Mergui; he complained to the English captain about the action, which contravened what was indicated in the letter to the King of Siam, namely to wait sixty days before proceeding to acts of hostility. There was no reply other than what had been done was done. However, the Siamese officers at Mergui sought justification for this action of Mr White; he thought to assuage them by telling them it was an affair between him and the captain, and that the captain would make amends. These officials, having waited some days and things remaining the same, took their own measures and decided on the action which they undertook.

One evening when Mr White was escorting the English captain (who was coming from supper at his house) back on board his longboat, they were attacked by a troop of Siamese who were lying in wait for them to do them harm. The captain received a sabre cut on his shoulder; Mr White, in his dressing gown, followed by a few armed Englishmen who served as guards, wanted to return to his house and assemble the Europeans scattered in their different lodges. He learnt that the Siamese had already seized his house and placed a strong guard at the gate, which fired on him and his men. His guards replied in kind. However, realizing from the noise and firing which could be heard in several places that the alarm had been raised throughout the town, Mr White found he could do nothing else than try and save himself; he returned to the river bank, met the wounded captain who was coming to join him and had not been able to embark; they forced their way past the body of Siamese who opposed them, jumped in the longboat and reached ship. The noise they heard afterwards from land, together with the discharge of cannons and muskets, the fires which they saw coming from Mr White's lodge and several other houses belonging to the English, left them in no doubt that every national was being attacked.

The following day, as their vessel went to join the two other ships which the captain had seized, they saw the bodies of five Englishmen which the tide had carried out to sea. They had many wounds and were entirely disfigured with blows which had been inflicted after their death. To savage in this way the bodies of their enemies is in the nature of almost all peoples in the Indies, but especially the Siamese, who are more cowardly, base, and servile than most when they are conquered, but are cruel and barbarous when they have the upper hand. Some people told a different tale: that Mr White was attacked when he was supping at table, and he escaped through an unguarded exit; but I am writing what I know of the true story given in personal communication.

Mr White did not believe for a moment that the King of Siam or Mr Constance had given orders for this massacre, but that the

Siamese officials of Mergui and Tenasserim had undertaken it on their own initiative after the seizure of the King of Siam's vessel and the harm done to his subjects, and who waited in vain for recompense. They and their families would have been undone if they had not sought means of reasoning with the English captain with whom they believed Mr White was in collusion, given the good relations the two appeared to maintain. Since then, though, it was learnt that Mr Constance was not satisfied with the conduct of Mr White. This person conducted all the trade on his own account; only he could accept goods brought from outside to Mergui, no local merchant dared to interpose; he set the prices according to his whim both for buying and selling. He was accused of frequently insulting the local people, and of having personally profited almost exclusively from the prizes seized by the King of Siam's vessels. It also seemed probable that he used other means than commerce to amass in four or five years a considerable estate: he had sent goodly sums to England, he still had plenty on his vessel, and he confessed to us that he had left in his lodge more than 100,000 *écus* in Japanese gold cupangs and in Siamese silver ticals. It is said that he had refused several times to go to Siam [Ayutthaya] after receipt of letters from Mr Constance who wrote to summon him thither; he was afeared that he would have to give account and, according to some, that, following this refusal, orders had been sent from Siam to Siamese officials who were not disposed in his favour. What seems to confirm this thought is that the Siamese officials who perpetrated the massacre after being arrested, placed in irons, sent to Siam [Ayutthaya] and cast into prison, were subsequently released without suffering any other punishment. It is thought that the King of Siam had only acted out of prudence in having them arrested, to try and persuade the world that he had nothing to do with this event. But there were those who maintained that there were secret orders to attack the English, and particularly Mr White who was suspected of being in collusion with the officials in Madras to make them masters of Mergui. Mr White told us that there were 150 Englishmen in Mergui at the time of the massacre. Almost all of them perished, even two or three Frenchmen who were there with them and whose nationality could not be distinguished in the heat of the action.

Mr White placed all the blame for the rupture between the English Company and the King of Siam on the officials of the Madras government, their desire to amass wealth by any means, sometimes very base and shameful. The cause of the King of Siam being brought to break with them was on account of some gems which this monarch had ordered them to buy for him. They were sent to him with a just single-line bill, so many gems costing 10,500 pagodas [a coin worth about 7 shillings]. The King of Siam after receiving them had their value estimated. Dutchmen who were well-versed in such matters were employed, as well as local people, and Sieur Véret. The highest estimation was for 4,250 pagodas. An official of the English Company charged with this commission was informed, but no ajustment was made. The King of Siam then sent them to the directors in London, so as to demonstrate the bad faith of their chief officials.

Mr White told us that when the ship from Madras anchored at Mergui, the King of Siam's vessel, which the English captain seized, was loaded with victuals and water for the journey to England which this monarch had resolved would be undertaken to bring his complaints to the Company's headquarters. A considerable sum should have been placed aboard, to be used in buying up European goods for the return journey.

After Mr White and the English captain had rejoined these two vessels, that which belonged to him was returned to him after the captain had received several thousand ticals in recompense. Some said the sum reached 30,000. The other two ships set sail for Madras. Mr White remained for two or three months among the islands which lie before the port of Mergui, waiting for a boat to enter the port in order to write to Mr Constance. As none appeared, he set sail for Aceh to take on victuals, and then anchored on the coast, in the roads of Narsapour, Palicate, and finally in Pondichéry. He told us his plan was to go to England and inform the king and the Company of the faithless conduct of the Company's officials in Madras, but particularly for having broken through base interest with the King of Siam where the English nation was held in high esteem, several Englishmen being employed in the service of this monarch and where they had made considerable fortunes.

This is what we learnt from the meeting we had with him, and, given our knowledge of the conduct of the officials in Madras, he was fairly exact in what he related. It should be added that the tart letters sent by these gentlemen to Mr Constance and the like replies they received had considerably embittered both sides. Mr White had come to Pondichéry to take on victuals and refreshments for his journey; the poor condition of the country was against this, and in addition we had need of what we possessed for the ships we were expecting from Siam [Ayutthaya] and Mergui. We gave him two and a half thousands of rice, which is all we could spare. We were obliged to him for the help he had given to the officers of our Company's ships which had travelled to Mergui when he was the administrator or receiver of customs.

At nine in the evening on the same day, 15 January, three cannon shots were heard in the roads; Mr White was afraid it was a ship from Madras sent in pursuit of him. We knew that there was one plying the coast and the officials in the government were not counted among his friends. We learnt on the return of a catamaran which we sent to the roads that it was the ketch the *Saint-Joseph* returning from Bengal. That made him feel better; he embarked at the same time and set sail on the 16th at dawn. We learnt subsequently that he landed in Ireland, not daring to go straight to England, without assurances that he would be well received there. Whilst he was waiting for replies to letters he had sent there, death overtook him and ended his travels and his transactions. (II, 510–515)

The background to this long account is well known. The East India Company's officials were less than models of probity, and most were trading on their own account. George White, Samuel's brother, was the captain of the *Hopewell* which in 1670 had taken Phaulkon on his first journey to Asia. Richard Burnaby, accompanied by Phaulkon, arrived in Ayutthaya about 1678. The two White brothers, Burnaby, and Phaulkon were all involved in underhand trade, since royal monopolies operated for nearly all exports. Phaulkon, once in power, rewarded his old trader friends; Burnaby was made governor of Mergui, and Samuel White *shahbandar*, alternately translated as harbour master or receiver of customs duties; the two functions went together. From Mergui they continued their operations and grew immensely rich. The East India Company regarded them as pirates, along with many non-Company English operators. Burnaby and White offered lavish entertainment to Captain Weltden, commander of the *Curtana*, accompanied by the *James*, who had arrived from Madras on 23 June, hoping to temporize, but the Siamese suspected collusion, and on 14 July attacked every Englishman in sight. The *James* was sunk by the Siamese firing shore batteries, Burnaby was killed along with some sixty other Englishmen, and White left on his ship, the *Resolution*, managing to persuade Weltden to let him sail for England. He did not die in Ireland, but suddenly in Bath, in April 1689, only six months after his return.

Martin's account, giving White's viewpoint, with occasional comments of his own, is extremely valuable in this murky affair. It also throws light on the dispute between King Narai and the Company. However, apart from the necessity of maintaining good relations with the East India Company officials in Madras, the massacre had little effect on French trading operations, and indeed, a Frenchman, Beauregard, was nominated by Phaulkon as governor of Mergui in August 1687. We shall come across this unfortunate young man on further occasions.

CHAPTER SIX

THE LA LOUBÈRE-CÉBERET EMBASSY, 1687

THE first news recorded by Martin of the second French embassy to Siam reached him in August 1687.

The Company vessel the *Président* dropped anchor on the 6th in our roads. We learned by the packets addressed to us of the departure from Brest of a squadron for Siam under the command of Mr de Vaudricourt, former naval captain. The squadron consisted of two frigates of fifty pieces [of cannon], three store ships, and another small frigate called the *Maligne*. Mr Desfarges was one aboard these vessels; he is a lieutenant-colonel in the Queen's Regiment, a lieutenant of the king in Brisach, and named by His Majesty camp marshal and commander of the troops embarked on the vessels, comprising ten companies, each with ... [blank] men and their officers, and Mr de Bruant, second to Mr Desfarges, as brigadier. Mr de Vertesalle was nominated governor of Bangkok; there was a major general, a commissioner general, arms and the necessary munitions for the troops. Mr [de] La Loubère and Mr Céberet, envoys extraordinary of the king to deal with the King of Siam and his ministers, were with the squadron, as well as the Siamese ambassadors who had gone to France with the Chevalier de Chaumont, fifteen Jesuit priests under their superior Fr Tachard, and the Abbé de Lionne with some Missionaries. The sending of the squadron to Siam was not only to assure the Company's commerce, but was also in the light of the propositions made in France by the ambassadors or else in letters which Mr Constance had written; this was not known to us at that time. There were orders for Mr Deslandes to go to Mergui and thence to Siam [Ayutthaya] where it was likely that he could notably contribute to the advantage of trade through the knowledge he had of that kingdom, resulting from the stay he had made there, as well as to turn to advantage the commercial treaty which he had drawn up with the ministers of the King of Siam. (II, 489–90)

This was considerably more than an embassy, almost an occupying force. Martin would have been unaware of the secret instructions given to Tachard which virtually made the envoys useless and which were to cause such friction throughout the duration of the embassy. He also would not have known at this juncture that Desfarges had instructions to occupy Bangkok by force if it were not freely handed over. He must surely have suspected that ten companies of soldiers were not sent merely in support of the two envoys, and the fact that de Vertesalle was apparently appointed from Versailles to be governor of Bangkok (be it just the fort or the whole province) must have indicated a military manoeuvre of considerable extent.

Five months later (in fact, after the embassy was concluded), Martin recorded further news of the embassy, with the arrival in Pondichéry of the French navy ship the *Oiseau* on 19 January 1688, commanded by Mr Duquesne.

I received a letter from Mr Céberet: he advised me he was sending the vessel in advance to bring us five barrels of silver, to be brought ashore. The *Saint-Louis* was to set sail with 100,000 *livres* aboard for Masulipatam, to take on goods there with this sum, and then to proceed to Mergui, where he would embark on the *Président*, to travel afterwards to Pondichéry. I received letters from Mr Deslandes on the state of affairs and the negotiations in Siam. I shall speak of this later. (II, 516)

The *Président* was due any time, but was preceded with confirmation of the events the previous July in Mergui.

> On 24 January, a small galot anchored in the roads. I sent someone on board and a Dutchman came ashore. He told us he had left Mergui in this vessel with the *Président* on which Mr Céberet and Mr Deslandes had embarked, that the galot was captained by Sieur Mainferme who had served the Company in divers positions and who had died in the crossing. There was tin and rice for us on board this small ship. The Dutchman was present at the Mergui massacre, from which he had happily been spared. He recounted the event in almost the same terms as Mr White had already done. The principal personages who were massacred and of whom we had received confirmed news were Sieur Burnaby, governor of Mergui, Captain Lesley, who commanded the King of Siam's vessel which had many times dropped anchor in our roads, two English officers, and a Dom Joseph, a Spaniard known to the traders on the coast. (II, 517)

The *Président* arrived the following day. Martin naturally went on board to receive one of his Company's directors, and Céberet came ashore with him, to be lodged in accommodation which Martin and his wife normally occupied (II, 517). There follows a lengthy account of the difficulties faced by the La Loubère-Céberet embassy to Siam.

> It would be a long recital to reveal all of what happened in Siam on the arrival of the envoys, the king's troops, and the negotiations which took place there. So many persons intrigued and became involved in these affairs according to the roles they played and are consequently so opposed to those who relate them, that it would be difficult for someone not on the spot to unravel their different actions. I shall only write what I know and what is known, leaving all the details and what occurred in more private moments to the persons who took part in these events.

The squadron had a good journey, and took on victuals at the Cape of Good Hope and Batavia. The gentlemen envoys went ashore in this capital, but incognito; perhaps they had foreseen that by revealing who they were, they would not have received due recognition of their rank. The Rev. Fr Tachard who brought along twelve [fifteen, as stated earlier, though one died en route] Jesuit priests went ashore: he went to greet the governor-general, but was not as was well received as on his first voyage [in 1685]; the governor excused himself for his Company's orders and for other particular reasons which led him to request the Reverend Father as well as the other Fathers to avoid walking in the town, and even advised him to withdraw. The journey to Siam was resumed. It is said that from the first days after their arrival, the chief characters were in dispute. As there were differing interests of religion, the army, and trade, each sought to limit the advantages accruing to the other. However, the envoys were received with all the honours which could be expected of their rank. (II, 518)

Martin's account of the journey at this point glosses over the heavy loss of life which occurred among the French soldiers en route to Siam. The reason for Tachard's cool reception in Batavia was to be found in the revocation of the Edict of Nantes in 1685, which led to a massive exodus of Huguenots from France: the Jesuits were plainly unwelcome in an outpost of a bastion of Protestantism. The disputes which occurred among the "chief characters", which have been plainly revealed in the recent publication of Céberet's account of the mission, were entirely due to the arrogance of Tachard vis-à-vis the legitimate envoys La Loubère and Céberet; he claimed he had secret orders (which he refused to show the two envoys) from the Marquis de Seignelay, Secretary of State for the Navy, which placed him in charge of the mission. A further cause of dispute was due to the two envoys being nominated "envoys extraordinary", but they were not accredited with the title of ambassadors.

It is said that Mr Constance was much surprised by the arrival of the troops, which he had not expected; he had only asked for fifty or sixty Frenchmen to place in the chief posts in the kingdom of Siam and in the positions of greatest importance. In France, apparently, other views prevailed about the sending of troops, to be assured by their presence about this minister, the sincerity of whose propositions was held in doubt. The greatest problem for Mr Constance was the declaration made to him, on the part of our king, placing French troops in the fortress of Bangkok to secure it and to do the same at Mergui. There was no problem with Mergui, the place having already been offered, but with regard to Bangkok, it was remonstrated that the people would grumble if it were placed in the hands of foreigners. However, as the court's orders were to take possession of this stronghold and even to use force if it were refused, Mr Constance managed the King of Siam so well that this monarch gave him a free hand. What helped in the matter was that he had a particular affection for our nation. The troops entered the stronghold and little time was lost in establishing fortifications which had been decided upon for it.

The troops had left France numbering ... men [blank: the squadron carried in all 1,361 persons, of which 636 were soldiers and officers]. Some ... [blank: 154] died en route. The commander, as I have already remarked, was Mr Desfarges, formerly lieutenant-colonel of the Queen's Regiment, then the king's lieutenant-colonel in Brisach, whom His Majesty had made general in charge of this expedition. His deputy, Mr de Bruant, had been major...[blank] and was made brigadier for this expedition; Mr de Vertesalle, appointed as head of the government of Bangkok, when he received orders to embark on this occasion was major in the regiment of ... [blank]. The personalities of these gentlemen were very different. Mr Desfarges, an old hand and a good soldier, who had demonstrated his prowess in several encounters, most particularly in the battle for Cassel where he contributed much at the head of his regiment both by his fighting qualities and by his conduct at this great victory; this action in which he distinguished himself brought

67

him the esteem of Monsieur [Louis XIV's brother] and recognition for a recommendation to this prince of an abbey for one of his sons, and later the king's lieutenancy at Brisach to take some rest from his exertions. Mr Desfarges having spent all his life under the colours, having entered the army when 15 or 16 years old, had perhaps neglected the other talents which would have been necessary for him in such a distant enterprise as that in Siam, with a broader understanding of political governancy where he had to conduct himself with foreigners and keep the French in order. This deficiency which he well recognized made him fall into another error, in believing people who were clever enough to insinuate themselves into his good graces and who often caused him to take inappropriate action by their lack of understanding of the matters they wished to meddle in, or by raising themselves to the position of advisors. Mr Desfarges also appeared extremely covetous, and he did not sustain with sufficient brilliance the position with which the king had honoured him. (II, 518–520)

Martin chooses his words carefully to summarize Desfarges' limited virtues and extensive limitations, including his ignorance and cupidity. The *Chronologie historique militaire...* of N. Pinard (Paris, Herissant, 1760–1778, 8 vols) lists Desfarges' early career, but fails to give his first name, only the inital N., and also fails to give his date of birth and background. Probably born about 1645 (and thus about 42 on leaving for Siam), he was made captain in Cardinal Mazarin's French infantry regiment in March 1661, and saw action in the sieges of Bergues, Furnes, Courtrai, and Oudenarde in 1667 and in Franche-Comté in 1668. He was promoted lieutenant colonel in his regiment, renamed the Queen's Regiment, in November 1670, and saw action in Maastricht in 1673, Seneffe in 1674, the sieges of Dinant, Huy, and Limburg in 1675, and Condé, Aire, and Bouchain in the following year. The battle of Cassel, mentioned by Martin, and the taking of Saint-Omer, took place in 1677, and the year after Desfarges was also a participant in the siege of Ypres and the battle of Saint-Denis.

Desfarges resigned his position in the Queen's Regiment when he was made the king's lieutenant in Brisach on 10 January 1683.

Brisach is now Breisach-am-Rhein in Germany, opposite the town of Neuf-Brisach which was only founded in 1699 as a consequence of the Treaty of Ryswick in 1697, under which the territories on the right bank of the Rhine were ceded by Louis XIV. Old Brisach, as Breisach is sometimes known, was French from 1648 to 1697.

Desfarges was promoted "maréchal de camp" (brigadier) in January 1687 to command the king's troops about to be sent to Siam. As he was the most senior French military person in Siam he was usually referred to as general. He was granted 15,000 *livres* in emoluments, and also 4,000 *écus* for his retinue; these were handsome sums, coming to some $110,250 and $88,200, using 1995 gold price conversions. They were not, however, sufficient for Desfarges, who was to be widely suspected of misappropriating funds for his own use. Certainly two of his sons, the Marquis and the Chevalier Desfarges, spent freely of their father's fortune in Martinique after their father's death at sea on the *Oriflamme* on returning to France in 1690, as Challe indicated in his *Journal d'un voyage fait aux Indes orientales (1690–1691)*.

> Mr de Bruant had the reputation he had acquired under arms of having a clever, discerning mind, who knew much, but was extremely difficult to converse with in agreement for any length of time; his great fastidiousness caused him to observe even the smallest details of persons' movements; extremely mistrustful, he was not liked by his officers for the difficulties he raised in accommodating his friendship; he demanded the submission of subalterns and a great deal of deference. He was due to go to Mergui with the troops, but I do not know if this was an order from the court [at Versailles] or a decision taken in Siam.
>
> Mr de Vertesalle was well versed in the arts of war, he was most particular in observing all the regulations, but stubborn in his

opinions which he did not change readily; he spent the emoluments he received from our king on his table, at which the officers were welcome and he was liked by them. He was the only one of the officers who did not leave Bangkok, where he remained ever carrying out his functions. He was not liked by Mr Constance who thought he was proud or scornful for not going to Siam [Ayutthaya] to pay his respects, although this was only carrying out the duties he had been charged with. There was also some trouble with the naval officers and it was said that letters had been written to France against him.

It is not necessary to indicate the character of the envoys extraordinary. Apart from the fact that these gentlemen did not stay there long, their merit is sufficiently well known. They brought for Mr Constance the Order of St Michael which our king had conferred on him, as well as the rank of count. The envoys found in this minister many difficulties in their negotiations. Mr de La Loubère, of a more fiery temperament than Mr Céberet, lost his temper in some meetings, which caused a kind of rupture between Mr Constance and him and which could not be entirely repaired. Mr Céberet, with a gentler, insinuative nature, got on better with the minister, though he abandoned not one jot the interests he was charged with defending. As he had to pass by the [Coromandel] coast, he hastened the business to be conducted. Finally the treaty was concluded, one rather better than that determined by the Chevalier de Chaumont; but it only affirmed the articles which Mr Deslandes had agreed on his departure from Siam for Surat. Mr Céberet, perhaps foreseeing new difficulties, left immediately after the treaty was concluded and Mr Deslandes with him. The first of the three [Siamese] ambassadors made a point of accompanying him as far as Mergui. This ambassador, who had been showered with honours in France and appeared much in favour of our nation, changed his views after his return to Siam. It is said he was vexed at not being allowed to travel in the first boat to go ashore which carried the Rev. Fr Tachard; it seems also that it was his due, he being charged with the negotiations. His resentment redoubled when he was badly received by Mr Constance and also because he had not been able to see the king before the departure of Mr Céberet. This curious conduct in the dispositions of the minister was planned, but it contributed greatly, according to what was said, to the events which I shall relate in their time. (II, 520–521)

Thus Martin sets the scene with the principal characters, all of whom he was to know well personally, with the exception of La Loubère, Phaulkon, and Kosa Pan, the first Siamese ambassador to France; and these three he knew sufficiently by repute. Desfarges lacked education and subtlety, de Bruant (sometimes known as du Bruant, but always referred to by Martin as 'Sieur de Bruant') was overweening and proud, de Vertesalle was stubborn and preferred the company of his officers to grovelling before ministers, La Loubère was hot-tempered, Céberet tried to calm things, Tachard pushed himself forward, all-powerful Phaulkon, now a count of France, busily played his own game, and Kosa Pan was furious with him, probably seeing through his plans.

Given this discoordinate assembly of characters, it is hardly surprising things went wrong. Just how wrong will be seen.

Martin continues his account of the embassy from a distance:

Readers may be surprised at the return of Mr Deslandes after having received orders from the court to go to Siam; it was known that he was much esteemed there by the king when he was head of the Company's factory there, and as Mr Constance was not then in the high rank which he afterwards reached, a bond of friendship arose between the two which was thought in France would contribute to the advantages of our nation. The sentiments of the minister changed with his fortune, he was irritated with us because we did not treat him as His Excellency in the letters we had written to him, we had only employed ordinary terms, not being able to foresee he would be given another title. This reason, but which perhaps only served as a pretext, was in part the cause for the return of Mr Deslandes. Yet another was suspected. As he was still appreciated by the King of Siam, and this monarch had even asked pressingly that he remain, it was thought that there was some jealousy and, together with other subjects which it is not appropriate to discuss, he refrained from staying in a place where he foresaw that there would inevitably be many subjects for discord. Mr Constance however treated him very civilly. We learnt that this minister was to enter the Company for 100,000 *écus* in the position of director-general. (II, 521–2)

What these inappropriate 'other subjects' were it is impossible to do more than guess; it may be that there were some disagreements over Phaulkon's trading ventures, though these would surely have been in order to be discussed by Martin. He hints at something less than honourable, but he is, after all, talking about his son-in-law. The comment is mystifying, but possibly refers to Phaulkon's life as a libertine before becoming respectable and marrying. Martin resumes:

During the envoys' stay in Siam [Ayutthaya] or Bangkok, their good reception, feasts, and local divertisements were almost continual; the officers and the troops, even the crews of the vessels, were always fed at the expense of the King of Siam. Everything was done honourably; almost all the officers received presents. Yet those with an understanding of the country already foresaw the changes which subsequently occurred there.

Sieur Véret had paid a visit to Borneo, where he had taken some 12,000–15,000 *livres* of goods which he had sold on credit to a local potentate; he was preparing to return this year to go and obtain payment. He had very grand ideas for an establishment on that island. It was thought that there was more imagination than solid fact in his proposals. It was a sequel to what he had written to Mr de Seignelay and the Company. As I had been careful not to become involved with the different interests concerning Siam, I shall only relate what I have learnt. (II, 522–3)

Martin in January 1688 records the death in Siam of Abbé Pallu of the Foreign Missions, who had gone to the Indies to visit the Missions (II, 522–3). Trade continued, but was still closely linked with Siam: the *Oiseau* was ready to set sail at the end of the month, loaded with bales, including the goods sent by Phaulkon which had remained in the French stores from the previous year (II, 523).

Céberet sought Martin's advice about returning overland to Surat, visiting the Great Mogul and travelling on to Persia. Martin advised against it, as all the countries he would be passing through were at war. Céberet therefore decided to return directly to France on the French navy ship, the *Oiseau*. Scarcely had Céberet set sail that a packet arrived from Pilavoine, the director of the French factory in Surat, with several letters for the Company director attempting to persuade him to pass through Surat, but the *Oiseau* was already more than two leagues from the roads (II, 523–4). Though Martin does not say so, Forbin travelled on the same ship to Brest, where the ship arrived on 18 June; Forbin in his memoirs says that he and Céberet compared notes about Siam, and the duplicity of Phaulkon.

Intra-country trade in rice and tin continued. The *Saint-Louis* offloaded Siamese rice in Masulipatam, and the royal supply ship, the *Normande*, arrived on 9 March with more rice, tin, and tuteneg. It also brought further news from Siam.

The poor relations between Mr Constance and Mr de La Loubère had worsened after the departure of Mr Céberet. The [French] ships had brought two mortars of a new type which had been invented in France, several bombs, and twelve bombardiers to make them work; it was thought they would be used against Bangkok if the King of Siam refused to hand this fortress over to the French. When Mr

Constance knew about these two mortars, he sought pressingly to have one put ashore to demonstrate it to the King of Siam his master, who was curious to know how it was constructed. Mr de Vaudricourt, captain of the *Gaillard* and commander of the squadron, had been given strict orders from our king to bring them back to France and also to bring back the bombardiers. Mr Constance had made several insistent requests [for them] to this commander who had always excused himself on account of his orders. Some persons intervened and had the envoys write to Mr de Vaudricourt to give satisfaction to the King of Siam. He gave in, one was put ashore and then taken to Louveau [Lopburi], where I believe it was tried out. Mr de La Loubère asked for its return before his departure to take it with him; after several postponements he was categorically refused and told it would not be returned. This is what angered him still more with Mr Constance, the more so as Mr de Vaudricourt made him answerable for this to the king, as well as for the bombardiers, some of whom also remained in Siam. The departure of the envoy from the minister was brusque and the occasion of sharp words. Mr de La Loubère left immediately, went to Siam [Ayutthaya], travelled to the mouth of the river, and embarked on the *Gaillard*. The Rev. Fr Tachard who was to return to France as an envoy to the pope and to our king and loaded with more presents, delayed embarking while waiting for letters from Mr Constance; Mr de Vaudricourt was for leaving promptly. After several protestations, and when about to set sail, the Reverend Father arrived on board with several mandarins and some Tonkinese who were claimed to be Christian deputies from the Kingdom of Tonkin travelling [to France] to request Jesuit priests. The king's ships set sail for their return to France on 3 January [1688].

The troops began to suffer in Bangkok; victuals which the King of Siam supplied ceased to arrive; soldiers went unpaid; several died. (II, 527–8)

The person who intervened in the matter of the mortar and the bombardiers may have been the ever-meddling Tachard, whose conduct throughout this embassy was reprehensible and whose collusion with Phaulkon was complete (he openly carried out Phaulkon's orders, to the point of transmitting messages to his cook in front of guests).

Tachard was accompanied by only three 'mandarins'—Ok-khun Chamnan Chaichong, Ok-khun Wiset Puban, and Ok-muen Pipith Raja—who were not given the title of ambassador, but were accompanied by several valets. They went with Tachard to meet Pope Innocent XI in Rome in December 1688, and King Louis XIV in Versailles in February 1689.

Thus ended the second French embassy to Siam. Céberet had done no more than re-establish the trading conditions which Deslandes had obtained several years earlier, La Loubère obtained nothing at all except the opprobrium of Phaulkon, whose power had gone to his head. But the French troops remained in Bangkok, and their position was to become still more difficult.

CHAPTER SEVEN

COMMERCIAL CONTACTS, 1688

FROM early 1688, Martin continued to note what appears to be growing trade from Pondichéry, particularly with Siam. In March he sent by a galliot going to Mergui a "substantial packet of letters for Siam addressed to the French officers in Mergui" (II, 530). But trouble with the English in Madras continued, understandably, since the French in Pondichéry appeared to be on good terms with Siam, whereas the English Company was at war with the country. The English had arrested a French trading ship, the *Saint-François*, but released it; the governor of Madras complained that "We gave the [French] flag to their enemies whom we protected; he meant the Siamese." Martin added "With the problems the English had with this nation, there was also jealousy regarding our establishment in the kingdom of Siam; they clearly foresaw that nothing could be done while we were on the same footing we then occupied." (II, 531) The English also maintained that the French ship the *Aigle* belonged to the King of Siam.

> The massacre at Mergui had not distanced the English from the kingdom; there were many [Englishmen] in Siam [Ayutthaya], several in the service of Mr Constance, even a secretary; these people passed on to Madras opinions which they thought useful to the service of their nation... (II, 531)

The secretary's name we know from Hamilton (1727) was Bashpool, though little more is known about him. Martin resolved that, should the English persist in their views over the *Aigle* and create an incident, he reserved the right to act according to law (II, 532). The ship in dispute arrived in Pondichéry in April, having "left Siam in a very poor state, without cables, anchors, and rudder..." In Aceh it failed to dispose of "goods which had been taken from the King of Siam's stores to send to France, but the ships which had gone thence were already filled with goods, and they remained. Sieur Véret thought they could be sold in Aceh." It was proposed to send the vessel to Mergui after "the April moon." (II, 534–5)

At the end of April the *Notre-Dame de Lorette* commanded by Sieur Duval, who had remained in Siam after disputes with the captain of the *Saint-Louis*, appeared in the roads, lacking cables and victuals too. The French merchant, Sieur de Rouen, came ashore.

> He had passed through Pondichéry last year and from there [travelled] to Siam for his [late] brother's affairs. He had little hope of obtaining satisfaction from Mr Constance, and decided to withdraw and return to Surat on the *Notre-Dame de Lorette*. (II, 537)

In May there appeared

> a small ship belonging to the King of Siam which loaded at Mergui to go to Bandar Abbas with envoys of this monarch aboard, to travel from there to the court of Persia with presents and trade goods. The French officers who had come from Siam [Ayutthaya] to Mergui also had effects on board to obtain wine and other refreshments from Persia. (II, 539–40)

The ship, commanded by one Boyer, had left Mergui on 10 February, but had run into every possible difficulty, mostly attributable to the captain. Boyer claimed at one moment the ship was French and another Siamese (both nationalities, as well as English, were on board). His commission turned out to be no more than a piece of paper from Véret and some Siamese mandarins. He was threatened with the rope round his neck, and Martin was fairly certain he intended to seize the goods on board in collusion with the other Europeans on board "who were no better than he." (II, 539–43)

There were more problems with Siamese vessels the same month. A large ship belonging to the King of Siam had left Mergui for Masulipatam, where it flew the French flag. It carried a commission from Véret and letters inviting the head of the French factory there to collude with the Chinese mandarins on board for a quick sale of the goods being carried. These included twenty-one elephants, tin, alum, and rice, all on the King of Siam's account, according to what was written. Martin disapproved:

> Véret, who apparently foresaw that all these dispatches of ships bearing the Company's commission and flag would lead to future business, defended himself by saying he was not master of the situation and was forced to subject himself to the will of Mr Constance... These dispatches of Siamese ships greatly embarrassed us for a time more than all the Company's other business. (II, 545-6)

A French vessel, the *Saint-Nicholas*, arrived in Pondichéry on 4 June with letters from the Company indicating an increase to twenty in the number of directors. Partially sealed letters came for Véret who was strongly condemned for his conduct "as we had foreseen". There were also packets for Mr Constance "addressed to the Count Phaulkon." (II, 547)

There were further problems with the Siamese ship in Masulipatam, which was unloaded all except for two elephants before the English got wind of its presence there. The Siamese mandarins offered them to the governor of Masulipatam, who refused them without orders from the court. Three elephants were to be sold and the profit, together with that from the sale of the tin, alum, and rice, was to be used according to the different instructions which "Count Phaulkon" sent to the head of the French factory at Masulipatam. This vessel was later unable to leave Masulipatam for lack of ballast (II, 558). A packet of letters from "Count Phaulkon" and Véret was sent to Martin.

> Mr Phaulkon charged us to acquire speedily the constructions he had sent plans for. Sieur Véret informed us that the Company's officials were in good health in Siam, that a plot had been discovered in Bangkok against the garrison, which was consequent on the Makassar uprising, and Dutchmen were suspected of entering into this plot, that the authors had been punished, that there was also the likelihood of a plot in Mergui against the French, but that the arrival of Mr de Bruant with troops at this stronghold had held the mutineers in check. (II, 550)

Martin wrote the first draft of this entry in June 1688; he was not to know for many months that by 5 June Count Phaulkon had been executed.

News in September came of the departure of the *Oriflamme* for Siam, with 350 troops to supplement those already at Bangkok, some officers, and money to pay the soldiers (II, 561); Martin was again not to know until much later that by 9 September the ship had arrived at the Bar of Siam.

The *Coche* set sail from Pondichéry for Mergui on 12 September loaded with cargo destined for Junk Ceylon and other goods intended for use in Siam.

> We inserted in the orders for the captain instructions to take all precautions before entering the port of Mergui, to establish whether

there were still Frenchmen there, and if they were masters of the place; we still thought that some change would occur in Siamese affairs. (II, 562)

The authorities in Madras sent Martin in September a copy of the King of Siam's declaration of war on the English; "it was abusive and full of passion" (II, 564) and undoubtedly the work of Phaulkon.

While Martin was preoccupied with improving the fortifications of Pondichéry, Siam caused him more headaches in November. The governor of Madras complained to Martin that the French crew of two vessels of the King of Siam lay in wait for English vessels travelling through the Straits of Malacca returning from China and Manila. "He complained of the conduct of the French who openly embraced the cause of the King of Siam against them." Another boat captained by a Frenchman left Mergui with a partly French crew for Aceh; there they found two English ships and tried to seize them by virtue of an order from the King of Siam against the English. Then a large English vessel from Madras entered port, was apprised of the French plan and prepared to seize the French-manned ship. This however, at the first cannon shot, being unable to withstand the attack of three ships, was run aground and the crew made off, though some were taken. The Queen of Aceh intervened by arresting the English, making them hand back the French prisoners, and the English made things up with the queen and her nobles by offering appropriate presents (II, 569–70).

Notwithstanding the English claims on the *Aigle*, Martin at the beginning of 1689 prepared to send the ship to Aceh and then to Ayutthaya to trade. But at this point the lack of speedy communications gives an air of unreality to the French Company's plans for Siam. Martin did not know it, but the French had already been forced to abandon both Mergui and Bangkok.

CHAPTER EIGHT

THE FRENCH EXPELLED FROM MERGUI, 1688

AS seen in the previous chapter, Martin suspected that events in Siam were moving to a climax in 1688 and had ordered the captain of the *Coche*, on approaching Mergui, to take every precaution in case of a change in the country's politics. In January 1689 he received the first confirmation that his suspicions were well founded. These came not from Ayutthaya or Lopburi, but from that part of Siam nearest Pondichéry—Mergui.

It was on 7 January 1689 that Martin had word from the captain of the *Coche*, Sieur d'Armagnac, of the "revolutions in Siam", and promised an account on his arrival in person. The ship anchored in the roads of Pondichéry the next day, and d'Armagnac came ashore.

We learnt from him that, after anchoring before the port of Mergui and in accordance with an article in his orders to enquire on the state of the French who had gone there from Siam [Ayutthaya], not seeing anyone come forward, he suspected some change. He took the precaution of taking some Siamese on board to be better informed, and was soon in hearing their account and then Sieur de La Touche's, who arrived at that time in Mergui from Siam, and who [also] travelled on the *Coche*. As there was little likelihood of leaving there to winter elsewhere, Sieur d'Armagnac, seeing he could probably remain in safety whilst being well prepared, decided to stay. The inhabitants of Mergui and Tenasserim were given the assurance that they had nothing to fear by coming on board, and some merchants came who dealt in the goods loaded in Pondichéry and intended for Siam. He made a reasonable profit on them. The crew did not lack victuals nor refreshments; the local people brought them in abundance. (III, 2)

He then set sail in December for Madras. Martin the same day received news that Mr de Bruant, General Desfarges' second in command, had reached Madras. La Touche, the ensign of the Siamese troops in Mergui, went to greet him, and give him letters he had from Desfarges.

Martin was clearly waiting for a fuller account from de Bruant, but in the meantime, on the 13th, a barge with twenty-seven soldiers in a pitiable condition arrived in Pondichéry, led by Mr Delaunay, navy lieutenant and captain of the French companies stationed in Mergui. He resumes:

> I shall here deal with the affair of Mergui; the account of the revolutions in Siam will appear in due course.
> After the arrival of the French in Mergui, Mr de Bruant, following his orders to construct a fortress according to a plan he brought from Siam, set to the work with all diligence. He bore letters for the mandarins of Mergui and Tenasserim who were required to provide all the workmen he might need. The plan drawn up for the fortress comprised an extensive piece of land, and the engineer who had designed it did not know the situation of the site; however, work was started on it. An engineer who had come from Siam with the troops was in charge. The workmen were at first provided by the mandarins according to the numbers requested; often they even assisted in bringing them to work. Some time after, a slowdown was observed in the work, and only some of the workmen came, then none at all. An explanation was sought of the mandarins with whom a very chilly relationship was evident for

some time. They gave reasons which were mere excuses, but which showed that they had received secret orders to act thus. Mr de Bruant not being party to them and receiving no letters from Siam suspected a reversal at court. Victuals began to run low, and the garrison was refused their supply, the French were badly treated, and it was learnt that the inhabitants of Tenasserim and nearby were assembling around Mergui.

During these movements, Mr de Bruant received a letter from Mr Desfarges. He informed him of an invasion of Siam being prepared by the Peguans or the Laotians. He told him to leave Mergui with all the French who were there under his command, to follow the mandarins who would be sent to him and who would serve as a guide to conduct him to the place where he expected him with the French whom he had withdrawn from Bangkok along with the Siamese troops. This letter, written in some disorder and confusion, was a clear indication that Mr Desfarges had been forced to issue this order, or that he explained himself in terms which lacked good sense to give the impression that a reversal had occurred at court. Mr de Bruant had no difficulty in understanding the import of the letter; he replied verbally that he would prepare to leave. He then called together the officers of the garrison and showed them the letter; but in the hope of receiving letters from the court which would enlighten them in greater detail on the state of affairs, they decided to take precautions against a local attack by constructing palissades of stakes and other obstacles in the places where they were most exposed.

The mandarins, recognizing by this conduct that the French suspected them and were perhaps informed of their intentions, felt that they had no further need of concealment, and declared themselves openly. The troops assembled around Mergui, numbering several thousands, appeared in a body, but were a rabble brought together in confusion, without discipline and some without arms. They nevertheless attacked the fort from which they were repulsed with losses. Victuals and water lacking, the well which had been constructed in the fort not being lined and filled with earth which had fallen into it, in this extremity Mr de Bruant called a council together. No other expedient was found but to withdraw and seize a frigate of the King of Siam in the port of Mergui and which bore its name. This resolution being taken, everything was prepared for departure at two or three in the morning.

This action was [later] held in France to be extraordinarily bold, but persons whose views can be trusted and who took part in the retreat were not in agreement with this opinion. They publicly stated that things could have been done at greater leisure and in greater order. There was indeed precipitation; twenty men were killed or drowned, including two officers, one being the engineer. The rest arrived at the frigate and set sail. Mr de Bruant found it desirable to remain some time among the islands that lie before the port of Mergui, waiting for some French ships. Victuals were lacking, they had to set sail, the vessel was poorly rigged, almost without ropes and anchors; they plied off the coast of Martaban, and then entered a river in Tavoy, in Peguan territory, without knowing its mouth or its depth, but necessity forced them to do so. After mooring a little within, they sent a longboat ashore where they saw some people assembled, to buy victuals; they were six Frenchmen in the longboat, including the Jesuit, the Rev. Fr d'Espagnac, and Sieur de Beauregard, who had been in the post of governor of Mergui before the arrival of Mr de Bruant. When they landed, following the customs of the kingdom of Pegu and other kingdoms in the [Burmese] dependency, they were arrested. Sieur de Beauregard, on the pretext of writing to the ship to get the other Frenchmen to come ashore too, which is what the natives wanted in order to seize them, warned Mr de Bruant that there was no safety for him in this river. Hunger drove them on, and he [de Bruant] resolved to escape. They found the natives had already begun to block the river with stakes close to its mouth to prevent them from leaving, a battery and armed persons on the bank fired on them as their ship approached. Our men replied by firing their arms with greater accuracy and intensity, which caused them to withdraw. They then forced the stakes and went out to sea, leaving on land Fr d'Espagnac, Sieur de Beauregard, and the other Frenchmen. They next set sail for Arakan, where they took strength with the assistance of a Frenchman established there for some fifteen or sixteen years, married, and wealthy. It was resolved to go next to Balassor [near modern Calcutta]; they met on the journey the *Lorette* which we had sent from Pondichéry for Mergui. This ship, fortunately for the French crew aboard, had met with contrary winds, and the vessel not being in a condition to outride bad weather, Sieur Duval, who commanded it, also put into Balassor.

The two ships set sail in convoy. Arriving in the roads, they found a squadron of English warships, the remains of their attack on Angely island. The commander of this squadron, by nature violent, sent to inspect the two ships; he was probably informed that they belonged to the King of Siam. He seized them. The action was easy: he had overwhelming strength. Mr de Bruant's explanations were dismissed. This brusque commander, who even the English consider brutal, ill-used an officer of the rank of Mr de Bruant; he made him go on one of his ships, with two captains, a lieutenant and some of the soldiers from the Mergui garrison and set sail for Madras. The rest of the soldiers under a lieutenant were put on board another ship. Mr Delaunay then came from Madras to Pondichéry with the soldiers who went ashore there as I have related.

Sieur de La Touche was in a redout at Mergui, commanding some Siamese. He was held there before the attack on the fort, and after the retreat of Mr de Bruant and the garrison. The mandarins inflicted their special torture, at which they are so adept; they were inspired by their hatred of our nation and to try to discover if any money had been hidden. Finally, tired of making him suffer without discovering anything, they sent him to Siam.

Mr de Bruant arrived on 15th with the Chevalier de Halegoit, naval lieutenant and captain of a company of troops. The relation of the action in Mergui was as I have given it, except for the retreat and some details of their destitution and the dangers to which they were exposed before arriving at the Arakan River. (III, 2–7)

Martin supplies no dates for the attack on the French in Mergui and their retreat, which took place on 24 June 1688 (van der Cruysse 1991: 474); de Bruant and his men therefore spent just over six months wandering around the Bay of Bengal. How La Touche returned to Pondichéry from Bangkok is explained later. Martin supplies no specific background to the two principal persons cheerfully abandoned in Tavoy to their fate by de Bruant, obviously more concerned at saving his own skin. About their fate we shall hear more. D'Espagnac was one of the Jesuits who had come to Siam with Tachard with the La Loubère-Céberet mission; he was presumably in Mergui to give spiritual succour to the troops, and was probably selected for the expedition to land in Tavoy because he spoke Portuguese. He served as translator between Tachard and Phaulkon after his arrival in Siam in 1687 (van der Cruysse 1991: 421). Beauregard, who according to Choisy (1993: 57) was not yet twenty in 1685 and had already seen several battles, was nearly killed in the Makassar attack on the Bangkok fort in June 1686, and miraculously recovered thanks to Forbin's ministrations (1997: 110–1). After Forbin took French leave from Siam at the end of that year, Beauregard was appointed governor of Bangkok in his place, according to the account of Céberet (1992: 54). After Burnaby, the English governor, and all his fellow-nationals had been massacred in Mergui in July 1687, Beauregard was appointed governor there until de Bruant arrived in February or March the following year.

De Bruant, before leaving Madras for Pondichéry, had naturally protested to the governor about the seizure of the *Mergui* and the *Lorette*. Martin was asked to send "persons of discretion" (he emphasizes the terms were those of the English governor) to discuss the matter. He adds that during de Bruant's stay in Arakan, six French soldiers deserted, reached the Coromandel Coast in a private trading ship, and had withdrawn to the English outpost at Congimer. De Bruant sent an officer to try to get them back; he returned with only three, the remaining three having fled, it was thought, inland.

This account of the events in Mergui in 1688 is clearly obtained from de Bruant, and with some later retouching. Martin hints that the French commander was less than brave in his conduct; the retreat from Mergui was certainly needlessly hasty, and de Bruant's abandoning of d'Espagnac, Beauregard, and four men at Tavoy was clearly reprehensible. But the retreat from Mergui was, as de Bruant suspected, due to a change at court. How great a change Martin was only to learn at the beginning of February 1689.

CHAPTER NINE

THE REVOLUTION IN SIAM, 1688

BY 8 January 1689 Martin was aware that his forebodings about a change in government in Ayutthaya were correct, but he did not receive full details from the participants until the beginning of February. On 1 February the *Siam* and the *Louveau*, "two ships supplied by the Siamese to transport the troops from Bangkok" arrived in the roads of Pondichéry. They landed not only soldiers, but several officers, Jesuit priests and Missionaries. The *Saint-Nicholas* anchored on 2 February, the supply ship the *Normande* on the 3rd, and the *Oriflamme* on the 4th at nightfall. Martin went aboard the flagship the next morning, and escorted ashore General Desfarges, who was on board, as well as more Jesuits and Missionaries on this ship (III, 8-9). Pondichéry, a small place, must have been crawling with clerics and military personnel.

His account of the "revolutions in Siam" then follows, with a clear disclaimer at the beginning concerning the motives of the different persons involved. His introduction also shows that the account was touched up some time later than February 1689.

> Before continuing in this account, I shall include here what I know of the revolutions in Siam; these are known and published facts. I shall not enter into what there is that is special or show

partiality. Apart from reports often being suspect because of the different interests of the parties concerned, I am not in a position to know what was contrary in the conduct of persons who had different sentiments, but I am persuaded that each believed he acted for the best. (III, 9)

Martin then rather compresses events, for Céberet left Lopburi for Mergui on 13 December 1687, arriving there on 1 January 1688, and returning to France on the *Oiseau*, which set sail from Pondichéry on 2 February; La Loubère, as we have seen, left the Bar of Siam on 3 January on the *Gaillard*, accompanied by the *Loire* and the *Dromadaire*. De Bruant did not leave Bangkok to take possession of the fort at Mergui until 17 February 1688:

> After their departure from Siam [Ayutthaya], the envoys and the king's ships set sail. Mr de Bruant went to Mergui with a detachment of troops. A little time later it was recognized, by muffled rumours which ordinarily precede important events, that something was disturbing the kingdom but which could not be discovered.
>
> Phra Petracha, one of the most important nobles at the court, a man of courage and enterprise, seeing the king nearly always sick, in advanced years and to all appearances unlikely to live long, sought the means of forming his clique. The king had two brothers, one scarcely capable of governing, and the other paralysed in all his members. (III, 9)

They were in fact half-brothers of King Narai: the elder, Chao Fa Aphaitot, was deformed and paralysed, and the younger, Chao Fa Noi, was the object of an intrigue in 1683 which Petracha apparently orchestrated, and on the king's orders was beaten by Petracha so severely, according to Fr de Bèze, that he was left for dead; he recovered, just, but without the use of his speech, which some said was diplomatic mutism. Neither was seen as a likely successor.

Petracha foresaw that he would have the French on his back in the enterprise that he was formulating, and that they would declare themselves for the successor nominated by the king. This monarch had brought up in close proximity to him a young man named Ok-phra Pet [Pi], the son of a mandarin, like an adopted son; rumour had it that the king would make him his successor by marrying him to his daughter, as he had no other children. Petracha brought into his clique the first of the three ambassadors [Ok-phra Wisut Sunthorn, Kosa Pan] who had gone to France; he was displeased with Mr Constance. Other mandarins also entered the plot, induced by the hatred of seeing a foreigner at the head of the government, Frenchmen in the chief positions, and perhaps also by the advantages which Petracha promised them. He also induced the main *talapoins*—these are the ministers of religion—causing them to fear the establishment of the Christian religion if the French remained. Petracha began to raise levies of people in the distant provinces and also to win over the Siamese officials who were in those parts. (III, 9–10)

Ok-phra Pi, sometimes Mom Pi, the son of Ok-khun Kraisitthisak, became Narai's favourite after the disgrace of Chao Fa Noi in 1683 and was always at his side. De Bèze (1968: 57) considered him of low birth and low intelligence, but he knew how to ingratiate himself into the king's good graces. The proposed marriage with Narai's only daughter, Kromluang Yothathep, was not to be; she considered him of too humble an origin for her. According to Fr de Bèze (1968: 87), eye-witness and confidant of Phaulkon, Petracha was close to the *sangha*, the Buddhist clergy, and was on particularly good terms with the head of all the monks in Lopburi, where the king preferred to reside. Martin resumes:

It was not difficult, in spite of all the precautions he [Petracha] took to conceal his plan, for these movements to create some comment. Mr Constance still had friends, he was informed and well knew that only Petracha could be at the origin of these movements.

He informed Mr Desfarges who did not leave the court, which was then at Louveau [Lopburi]. It was thought appropriate that the general should go to Bangkok to inspect the place, see how advanced the fortifications were and put everything in order before his departure. Mr Constance asked him if he could promise to return to court with a detachment of eighty or a hundred selected men when he wrote to him; he even added that he should state clearly if he saw any objection, so as to direct his request elsewhere if this relief was not forthcoming. Mr Desfarges, who had orders from our king to follow the minister's opinions, pledged this, and promised to return to court with the detachment on the first orders he received. He then left for Bangkok. (III, 10)

Desfarges was called to Lopburi by Phaulkon on 31 March to discuss the means of crushing Petracha's plot. He promised to return immediately with a detachment of men; he was warned by Phaulkon not to believe any rumours he heard of the death of the king (de Bèze 1968: 82, van der Cruysse 1991: 453).

Mr Constance, particularly warned of the movements in the provinces of the levy of troops and that he had no time to lose in carrying out the coup he had planned to rid himself of Petracha, wrote to Mr Desfarges to come to court with the detachment he had promised. This general left immediately with eighty or so men, officers, and soldiers, specially selected and capable of making a surprise attack. On his arrival at Siam [Ayutthaya], he informed Sieur Véret, the head [of the French factory], of his intentions. Sieur Véret, surprised at Mr Desfarges' journey, told him that the rumour of the king's death had filled the town, and the country was full of armed men; that he would find from between 12,000 and 15,000 troops on the road between Siam and Louveau who were waiting for him, that he would certainly perish, and that he felt obliged to give him this information: I relate the gist of what was said and done. Mr Desfarges, surprised for his part at this change of scenario, did not hesitate all the same in his intention to continue his journey. Sieur Véret, seeing him in this resolution, suggested he go to see the Missionaries. They were at the mission, and told him the same things, that he and his men would indubitably be lost if he continued, as well as the French who remained in Bangkok and in other places in the kingdom. This decided him to remain in Siam [Ayutthaya], but he also sent word to Louveau to be informed of the state of the city. Sieur Beauchamp, an army captain and aide-de-camp in Bangkok, and Sieur d'Assieux too, captain in the same detachment, went at different times; their report was that they had discovered no obstacle on the way, and the court was as tranquil as usual, the king was sick but still alive. They had spoken to Mr Constance, and to the Jesuits in Louveau, who assured them that there had been no change. Mr Desfarges was so strongly persuaded of the assembly of troops by the assurance of their existence which had been given him, and what was afterwards added, that the passage of two officers without encountering any obstacle was held to be a stratagem of the plotters to get him to undertake the journey and to lead him into ambushes which would be prepared for him. He decided to return to Bangkok, where he would withdraw with his men. (III, 10–11)

Desfarges had selected eighty-five soldiers and ten officers in Bangkok. Véret had just returned from Lopburi and so in theory knew the situation there. "The tales he [Desfarges] heard at the seminary of Constans' [Phaulkon's] bad faith as Minister of the Crown and of the scant credit he now possessed at court all went to convince Desfarges at last that Constans must be left to his fate." (de Bèze 1968: 88) One detail at variance with Martin's account was that only one officer was sent to Lopburi, at the suggestion of the bishop, and he was one Le Roy: he arrived at 1 a.m. on 16 April 1688 and found Phaulkon, his wife and the Jesuits calmly observing a lunar eclipse (de Bèze 1968: 84). Le Roy took a letter from Phaulkon, repeating his request that Desfarges take no notice of rumours, and come with his detachment of soldiers. But Desfarges' mind was made up; he decided to return to Bangkok (de Bèze 1968: 84).

This was the turning point of the whole imbroglio; Desfarges abandoned Phaulkon in spite of the specific orders of his king.

This conduct of Mr Desfarges, about which in France such diverse opinions have been [subsequently] written, is rather difficult to explain, given differing views as to whether his return to Bangkok was appropriate or if it would have been more advantageous to continue the journey to Louveau. Those who dissuaded him from continuing, by whom I mean the gentlemen at the mission, are of noted merit, of known probity and virtue, well versed in Siamese affairs after staying many years in the country, knowing perfectly the language and where they had gained friends who could be party to secret opinions. It is not to be doubted too that they were well persuaded themselves by what they told Mr Desfarges. However, the journey of the two captains to the court, and other details subsequently known, the report of people in the country (for there were those for and against) caused some to doubt the existence of this assembly of troops on the road from Siam to Louveau. It is certain that, if this advice had been ill-founded, the arrival at the court of Mr Desfarges with his men would have gained the field; Petracha would have been lost; by arresting him, it would have been safest to dispose of him at once. With the author [of the plot] dead, his clique would have dissipated completely; it would not have been difficult to secure the king's approval of the coup by providing testimonies from the mandarins implicated in his plot, who would have been seized and from whom would have been extracted the plotters' intentions, which were in complete opposition to the intentions of this monarch about his successor. (III, 11–12)

The return of Mr Desfarges to Bangkok triggered the beginning of the revolutions in Siam. It was reported that Mr Constance had hesitated to reveal to the king the intentions of Petracha. He was waiting to put things in readiness to oppose him before explaining himself to this monarch. He knew his violent and decisive character; he would explode and that would destroy all his neutralizing measures. But seeing the peril close, he disclosed the plot to him.

What happened was as he had foreseen; the king flew into a rage and issued orders for Petracha's immediate arrest. The rebel received report of this and gave him to understand there was no point in further concealment. Taking his decision [to act], he made himself master of the palace. News of this action, of a public uprising against the monarch, spread throughout Louveau and caused confusion everywhere. When Mr Constance received news of this, seeing his ruin assured, he too thought further dissimulation was pointless. It was said that by assembling the officers, the people who were close to him and friends he still had at court, he could have withstood and been in a position to withdraw or to die gloriously. But his judgment was at fault in this action, the most important in his life; it can be said too that the return of Mr Desfarges to Bangkok, by whom he thought himself abandoned, contributed greatly to this. He left his palace, followed by some English guards and a few French officers, including the two sons of Mr Desfarges. The Jesuits opposed his resolution for all their worth; their reasoning did not deflect him. As he did not doubt that Petracha had formulated plans for what remained of the king's life, he publicly declared that he wished to die defending a monarch to whom he had so many obligations, and, with that, like a man going to his death, he entered the palace. The door was closed on some of the people following him. He found Petracha there, the mandarins in his clique, and the people of their faction armed. He was arrested and disarmed, likewise the officers who accompanied him. He had a moment's conversation with the rebel; he was then taken to a platform in the palace, apparently to show the crowd that he was arrested, and then incarcerated. The Frenchmen did not see him again; the officers were kept under a strong guard, but without being mistreated. (III, 12–13)

Early in May the king had called his council together and announced his intention of nominating his daughter regent. Phra Pi tried to bring into the palace people in his (and the king's) favour; their entry was blocked by Petracha and his men. It was Phra Pi who then revealed the plot to Narai, according to de Bèze (1968: 87). Phaulkon was summoned, and confirmed everything. Narai exploded. Petracha brought out his supporters from the temples on 18 May in theory to defend the king against the foreigners. The palace was taken. The three French officers who went with Phaulkon to the palace were Beauchamp, de Fretteville, and the Chevalier Desfarges.

Petracha, master of the palace, the king, and Mr Constance, continued the same means to complete his crime; the most important was to get the French to leave Bangkok. He wrote to Mr Desfarges to return to Louveau where the king commanded him to come. It was said (but I am not certain about this) that it was indicated in the letter that this monarch had resolved to replace Mr Constance with him, and Mr Constance had been arrested for malversion in his duties. Persons at court wrote to Mr Desfarges not to undertake this journey; he was informed of the state of affairs and the plans of Petracha. As not all minds have the same opinions, some persuaded the general to go to court. I do not know what reasons they advanced but they were apparently strong, since he deferred to them. After having given his orders to Mr de Vertesalle for the safety of the command at Bangkok, he went to Louveau. Petracha received him proudly and like a person with all power in his hands; he spoke with indignation of the conduct of Mr Constance, the dissipation of the king's treasure and occasionally included the French in that. He moderated himself in time because of the assurances he gave that the same consideration would ever be shown them, but that, as they had come to Siam to contribute to the defence of the kingdom, on the information he had received of the movement of a body of Laotians, long-time enemies of the Siamese, and their entry into the country, Desfarges should write to the commander he had left in Bangkok to come to the court with the garrison, so as to go and confront the enemies together with the native troops who were assembled at the meeting point. Mr Desfarges, surprised at this proposal, held fast, and told Petracha that all the orders he might write to the commander he had left in Bangkok would be useless, he would not leave his post, and, if it were necessary to withdraw the garrison, it was absolutely essential that he should return. Petracha rejected this reply; both argued their point. Mr Desfarges stuck fast to his position, and finally informed the rebel that, leaving in Louveau what was dearest to his heart as a pledge for his word—speaking of his two sons—he should not doubt that he would return. Petracha, either because he thought that Mr Desfarges would carry out his promise or that preparations were not sufficiently advanced to bring things to a head, allowed the general to return to Bangkok. It was during this journey that the letter about which I have spoken when dealing with Mergui was written to Mr de Bruant.

Petracha had already advanced his business considerably but he could do nothing so long as there were persons who could dispute the throne with him. He began the tragedy with the death of Ok-phra Pi. This young man did not leave the king's bedroom, the only asylum where he believed himself in safety. He was taken from it though, either by deceit or by force, and then massacred. The king's two [half-]brothers were in the palace in Siam [Ayutthaya], and were brought out by the same means, put into sacks of scarlet cloth and beaten [to death] with sandalwood clubs. The timing of the death of Mr Constance was not known; it was not to be doubted that Petracha made him suffer all the tortures which are customary in the country. It is reported that he was taken outside the city at the beginning of night, and cut into pieces with blows from a sabre. The king died at the same time. We have definite information that the Dutch were heavily involved in these revolutions, particularly a certain Daniel in their lodge, a native of Sedan, and surgeon by profession, a convinced heretic and declared enemy of the Catholic religion and the French. It is also held by the same source for which there are testimonies that poison was added to a potion given to the king, which greatly hastened his death. I say nothing of the number of mandarins and other persons who were arrested during and after these revolutionary events; it is one of the common maxims of tyrants to dispose of people who are not of their faction or who could oppose their designs. (III, 13–16)

The Daniel referred to here was Daniel Brockebourde or Brouchebourde, a Dutch company doctor who in 1672 entered the service of King Narai, and the first of three generations of the family to hold the post of court physician (Brummelhuis 1987: 43). Though French, he was Protestant, and the effect of the revocation of the Edict of Nantes in 1685 was to drive him, as many others, into Dutch arms. He was accused by one Rigal of poisoning Narai on the orders of the director of the Dutch factory, Keyts, and Petracha (Sportès n.d. [1994]: 133–4 n.234). He was naturally detested by the French Catholics.

Phra Pi was beheaded on 20 May, but the death of Narai's half-brothers did not take place, in the matter correctly described by Martin, until 9 July; the bags and clubs were to ensure that no royal blood was spilt upon the ground. According to de Bèze (1968: 110) no one dared lift a finger in their defence, as Petracha had the support of the army and the "Moors". One detail that escaped Martin in his account is that when Desfarges arrived in Lopburi on 2 June, and Petracha saw that he made no move to defend Phaulkon, either in word or deed, the usurper assumed, correctly, the minister had been abandoned by the French; Phaulkon was speedily decapitated at Thale Chupson outside Lopburi on 5 June. Petracha visited the sick, imprisoned, and furious king a few days before his death, promising not to harm his half-brothers (de Bèze 1968: 107). King Narai died, according to de Bèze (who saw him two days before his death), on 10 July.

> Madame Constance was also taken; everything in her house was removed; she was tortured to reveal where her husband's effects lay hidden. She endured the torture with great resolution which astonished those who witnessed it; her greatest difficulty afterwards was to resist the brutal advances of Petracha's son. She was sent to

Siam, lodged in a stable, from whence she was taken to the palace to make preserves. Mgr the Bishop of Metellopolis was also arrested with several Missionaries and badly treated; everything in their houses was removed. The Jesuits were exempt of these persecutions; neither their persons nor their possessions were touched. The king, a little before his death, feared that they might be in need, and had sent each a catty, which is worth 150 *écus*. Petracha, after having completed the tragedy of Louveau, came to Siam to establish his court and gave orders to attack Bangkok. I did not learn the time it took for him to take the title of king nor for him to marry the daughter of the late monarch. (III, 16)

Mme Phaulkon was brought to Ayutthaya and worked as a servant in the palace, returning at night to her prison, while Sorasak, Petracha's son, tried to seduce her. Petracha had the late king cremated with the traditional honours, and had himself declared king the same day, 1 August, in Ayutthaya; his marriage to Princess Yothathep, heiress to the kingdom, took place about the same time, though she was said by de Bèze (1968: 111) to have a penchant for her father's now murdered younger half-brother, and to have spurned, understandably, Petracha's initial offer of marriage.

Thus ended the Lopburi *coup d'état*, with the death of King Narai (who may not have been poisoned, as Martin avers), Phaulkon, Phra Pi, and the king's two half-brothers; Yothathep was married off and immured, Mme Phaulkon tortured and imprisoned. Her troubles were not yet over, and those of the French troops in Bangkok were about to begin in earnest.

CHAPTER TEN

THE FRENCH RETREAT FROM BANGKOK, 1688

THE *coup d'état* removed all contenders to the throne including Phaulkon, had he really aspired to the crown, as some claimed. It did not remove the French troops from Bangkok, nor, immediately, those from Mergui. How the troops withdrew from Mergui has already been related. But Martin interposes two naval matters in his account here which are relevant to the events in Siam.

Some time before the revolutions, Mr Constance had ordered the arming of two of the King of Siam's vessels commanded by two French officers. A detachment of troops was embarked, led by a captain who was released from the main body. The common rumour was that these vessels were going to attack pirates roaming those seas. It was known later, from the instructions given to the officers, that their orders were to seize English vessels they met returning from Manila or which left Madras to go to these islands, but there was something even more objectionable: the officers were required by their orders to pass through the Straits of Malacca and to go to Madras, to burn all the ships they found in the roads there. I have already noted in this account the forewarning the English had of something of this plan. The passion of hatred or vengeance must have greatly goaded a man to require men of honour and the king's officers to undertake an enterprise in which their death was certain. People who were opposed to Mr Constance were surprised at the facility with which Mr Desfarges permitted the embarkation of the king's troops to wage war on the English, but either the officers on these vessels foresaw the little likelihood there was in fulfilling their orders, or the vessels were too poorly equipped to be able to pass the Straits of Malacca, for they remained a few months at sea, without meeting any ship, and perhaps they even desired this.

It was about this time that the revolutions occurred. As the troops were necessary for the defence of Bangkok, and boats were needed to be masters of the river and the sea, and as notice had to be given of the state of affairs to the Company's offices, in order to withdraw the necessities which would be required for the retention of the stronghold, it was decided to send off a small boat which Sieur Véret had prepared for a second trip he expected to make to the island of Borneo. This boat was to go and meet the two vessels which were on the high seas and also to wait for the ships expected from France, and inform the officers of the changes which had occurred in the kingdom of Siam. The naval ensign Sieur de Saint-Cry was ordered to command this small vessel; he was given some Frenchmen [to assist him]. He had not gone far from Bangkok when he was attacked by several Siamese barges; after a vigorous defence at a distance, Sieur de Saint-Cry saw they were prepared to board, and not being in a condition to resist them, given their large number, he had several grenades thrown on the bridge; the powder spread everywhere with trails to set light to them. He then withdrew to the wardroom with his men. The Siamese after boarding rushed to the bridge; the trails were ignited, the powder and the grenades had their effect, several of the enemy were burnt and wounded; those who escaped the flames withdrew in their barges or threw themselves into the river.

When the bridge was cleaned and the boats had withdrawn, Sieur de Saint-Cry continued his journey. The Siamese, apparently furious at seeing a small boat resist for so long, decided to board it a second time. Sieur de Saint-Cry realizing that there was little chance that he could escape, decided to blow the boat up. He had everything made ready for this; the numerous enemy leapt onto the bridge; the flames set to the powder cleared them from the boat and anyone nearby. The commander perished in this action; I heard it said that only a young French boy of thirteen or fourteen years was saved; he fell into some merchants' hands and suffered greatly during the time he remained thus. The losses on the Siamese side were considerable; it was even said that recognizing by this action the intrepidity and resolution of the French, having no concern for themselves when the loss of their enemies was of paramount importance, they were more guarded in their attacks. (III, 16–18)

Martin then returns to the situation in Bangkok itself, with the return of the two Siamese ships with French officers and troops on board. He inserts a rather tongue-in-cheek comment about the political abilities of oriental countries, and implies they are as good in tricking others as are western nations.

However the two vessels [mentioned above] returned to the roads of the river of Siam. Not enough consideration is given in France to the nations in the Indies for their ability and good sense; there are even historians who, when speaking of some of these nations, consider them as barbarians and savages. It is true that the first term well suits some because of their perfidy and cruelty, but it is certain that they are as intelligent in what concerns their treaties, their interests and their political governancing, and they have nothing to learn from European nations. The Siamese had foreseen the return of the two vessels; they held boats in readiness at the mouth of the river, with mandarins and refreshments on board. When the vessels arrived they went on board, and said the king was in wonderfully good health, likewise Mr Constance, and spoke of the well-being of the French in Bangkok (at that time they began to be treated in the manner I shall soon describe). The ships' officers readily believed all that they were told; the captain commanding the detachment of soldiers went on board the mandarins' ship and was taken to Bangkok, where he learnt all the changes which had occurred. Then there were orders either poorly issued or poorly understood which caused all the Frenchmen on the boats to be disembarked, to be sent to Bangkok, and the vessels remained in the hands of the Siamese. Mr Desfarges maintained he gave contrary orders, but the damage had been done and could not be made good. (III, 18–19)

Meanwhile, in Lopburi, those Frenchmen who remained were held hostage, but rather foolishly attempted to escape.

Mr Desfarges' two sons and the other French officers the general had left in Louveau when he made his last journey stayed there; they were restricted at the beginning of the revolutions and threatened, but then set free. They were even given permission to hunt. One day they went on horseback for this distraction, and resolved to advance to Siam [Ayutthaya] where they thought they would find means to take over a boat to take them to Bangkok. They were already half-way from Louveau to Siam when the Siamese realized their intention. They assembled a body of men to oppose their retreat; their numbers increased as the officers progressed and then closed in on all sides. They saw that there was no likelihood of going further. They were all well armed and some of them urged the others to force their path or to die gloriously. The more prudent thought it better to give themselves up; there were parleys between the two sides, and the officers consented to return to Louveau. But their sorry conduct resulted in their being required to hand over their arms to the Siamese. They were then seized; some were tied to the tails of their horses with people following with rattan sticks to force them to run at the same pace as the animals. An engineer died from this form of torture; the others arrived at Louveau in a state which is easy to imagine as a consequence of the treatment they had suffered, and they were locked up and closely guarded. (III, 19–20)

The scene then shifts back to Ayutthaya and Petracha's attempts to remove the French from Bangkok.

Petracha, not seeing the likelihood of forcing the French out of Bangkok and fearing the arrival of vessels which would give them the means of advancing to Siam, thought that diplomatic means would serve his purposes better. The first ambassador who had been to France [Kosa Pan] and was raised to the position of *barcalon* after the revolutions was to be the intermediary for this treaty. Each side entered into discussion, and it was finally agreed—which I shall relate at greater length in time—that the Siamese would supply the vessels and victuals for the departure of the French in Bangkok for Pondichéry. All that Petracha sought was to have the French out of his realm. There was a stay in the armed confrontation; the French were at liberty to go to Siam as when in times of complete peace. It was about this time that Sieur de La Touche, who had been arrested in Mergui, arrived at Siam; he brought the news of the retreat of Mr de Bruant on the frigate he had stolen from the port. The *barcalon* complained; he sought a letter from Mr Desfarges for the commander of the troops who had withdrawn from Mergui (and who, it was learned by letters, remained nearby among the islands) to return this vessel. The letter was written; Sieur de La Touche was the bearer. He returned to Mergui where he could learn nothing of Mr de Bruant, but where he found the *Coche*, and embarked. (III, 20–21)

La Touche is supposed to have written an account of events in Siam and the role he played, which Robert Challe said he was adding in his *Journal d'un voyage fait aux Indes Orientales (1690–91)* (Deloffre and Menemencioglu, eds, 1979: 478), but which for some reason was not included. La Touche clearly played an important role in the whole imbroglio, and it is a pity his record has not come down to us.

Martin then comes to the appearance of the *deus ex machina*, the *Oriflamme*, which as we know from chapter seven was sailing from

France to Siam with 350 soldiers on board and money to pay the Bangkok garrison.

Whilst everything was being prepared for the departure of the garrison in Bangkok, the *Oriflamme* dropped anchor in the roads at the mouth of the river of Siam. The Siamese had taken the same precautions as for the return of the two vessels; a barge went alongside with mandarins bearing refreshments. They again announced wondrous things about the King of Siam's and Mr Constance's health, and the good condition of the French in Bangkok. They were believed, not being able to foresee the changes which had occurred. Mr Cornuel, the second officer of the *Oriflamme*, got into the barge to carry the packets [of letters for the garrison]; he was accompanied by the first lieutenant and some officers sent from France to serve alongside the troops. They entered the river, but as it has many branches, the mandarins following their orders took a canal which took them away from Bangkok. Mr Cornuel, who had been twice to Siam, soon recognized that they were not passing in front of the places he had seen on other occasions; he spoke about it to the mandarins who gave him to understand they were taking a side and shorter route; finally they arrived in Siam [Ayutthaya] where they were surprised to see that they met with no Frenchmen and they were taken to the *barcalon*.

There were though some French officers from Bangkok in the town who had been sent to take charge of the victuals, the rigging and other things necessary for the voyage. Sieur des Rivières, a company captain, was one of them. On receiving notice of the arrival of a French ship in the roads and that there were some officers at the *barcalon*'s residence, he went there, entered a room where he found them and informed them of the changes which had arrived and the treaty [of capitulation] which had been drawn up. At the same time Mr Desfarges was informed of the arrival of the ships and the help aboard; he received by the same means the packets which were addressed to him. All this made no change to the state of affairs; the resolution which had been taken to withdraw was adhered to and all haste was made to depart.

The treaty required the French to abandon the fortress of Bangkok, and to withdraw the cannons, arms, and munitions which they had landed, and generally everything that belonged to them; they would leave with all honours which are observed in the most honourable capitulations; two approved vessels would be supplied with all necessities and the victuals which were needed to reach Pondichéry. The Company's factory would remain in Siam and all the commercial advantages and privileges in the documents agreed with the envoys [would obtain]. The two vessels would be returned from Pondichéry, and the Bishop of Metellopolis and Sieur Véret, the head of the factory, who were to remain, would be guarantors for the treaty and remain as hostages for the return of the two ships as well as for reimbursement of the payment which the Siamese had advanced for the acquisition of victuals and other necessities for the journey. Peace would be re-established in this way between the two nations and commerce open to the French in all Siamese ports. The Siamese also agreed to provide hostages for the execution of the treaty. (III, 21–22)

There then arose a great complication to the French plans for an honourable retreat: the appearance of the fugitive Countess Phaulkon at the fort at Bangkok. Nothing could be less honourable than the way she was treated by Desfarges, more anxious to save his skin than his reputation.

Mme Constance who was at Siam [Ayutthaya], informed that the French were to withdraw and fearing further ill treatment and persecutions of the Siamese, particularly from the son of Petracha, did not think that the precautions which had been taken for her well-being (by obliging the Siamese delegates for the treaty to promise that she would be allowed to live in peace with her family) were adequate for the pledges given, decided to withdraw to Bangkok with the one son still with her, flying our king's flag. She communicated her plan to persons in whom she thought able to confide. They apparently were not opposed to such a praiseworthy intention; this lady, or others on her behalf, spoke of it to Sieur de Sainte-Marie, an officer who was then in Siam, who offered his services. Persons being engaged and the boat being ready, Mme Phaulkon disguised herself, embarked with her son and the officer, and so travelled to Bangkok. The surprise of Mr Desfarges was extraordinary when he learnt of the arrival of this lady; he raged publicly against the officer, whom he had placed in irons, and Mme Phaulkon was locked up in a private house, with a guard at her door, so that no one could speak to her without his permission. Her escape was immediately known at the Siamese court; the French who were in the town were arrested and loud complaints came from the Siamese that the treaty was being contravened. The *barcalon*, who had done much for its conclusion, also made much ado, declaring that everything was in abeyance if this lady were not handed over.

Mr Desfarges assembled a council on the matter: Mr de Vertesalle and the captains of the troops constituted it. The general spoke heatedly of the action of Mr de Sainte-Marie for undertaking without orders the transfer of Mme Constance to Bangkok, exaggerated the consequences which he foresaw which would arrive from this form of abduction (but which most of the officers in the assembly did not think well founded), and then added that his view was to return her to the Siamese in order not to interrupt the execution of the treaty. It is to be noted that his two sons were among the captains, a third of these same officers was connected to him by a distant relationship, and a fourth whom he had won over to his side. These people supported his view to hand over the lady. It is maintained though that one of his sons, the Chevalier Desfarges, resisted, and only gave his vote at the end out of blind obedience to the desires of his father. Mr de Vertesalle, Mr de La Salle, commissioner-general of the troops, and the rest of the captains loudly maintained that she should not be handed over, that this lady had arrived flying the king's flag to implore his protection which had to be granted, that the honour of the nation depended on it, and it would be better to perish than to carry out an act which would cause other nations to berate us for, that Mr Constance had obtained from the king letters of naturalization, that His Majesty had even recently written letters which had arrived on the *Oriflamme*, saying that he took him and his family under his protection and that thus he and the persons dependent on him could be considered to be French, and there was both injustice and cruelty in refusing to this lady the asylum she sought and which was her due. Mr Desfarges did not appreciate this last opinion, and, not having been able to change the views of any of the officers, the council was dismissed.

This general then discussed the matter individually with his captains; he apparently thought he had changed their minds. The council was assembled a second time, but everyone remained resolved to keep Mme Phaulkon. Mr Desfarges did not fail to disregard this and declared he would hand this lady over to the Siamese and took responsibility for the matter himself.

As this matter has [since] caused much comment in France and persons of merit and distinction have been involved in the affair who were said to favour the general's view, I shall say what I know and what is generally known. The flight of Mme Phaulkon caused a great uproar at the Siamese court. People turned on the Bishop of Metellopolis, whose blameless life is revered by every nationality. Only the Siamese are sufficiently barbarous to bring themselves to inflict the violence and ill-treatment to which this great prelate was exposed during the siege of Bangkok and which he has been made to suffer since. After the threats which he and the Missionaries received to make them die in torment, Mme Phaulkon's family's turn came next; all her relatives were arrested, they were likewise threatened, and even all the Christians in Siam were included. The bishop wrote about this to Mr Desfarges; he explained to him that if it were decided to take this lady away, the cause of religion would be lost in the kingdom; he wrote as a pastor and a prelate who feared the loss of his flock, but his letter finished with an admission that not being competent in matters concerning the honour and reputation of the king and of nations, he deferred to the general, who should be more aware of them than him. I have seen the letter, I do not give the precise words, but their meaning; if there were secret conditions, I am not aware of them.

Mr Desfarges, having decided to hand over Mme Phaulkon and her son, informed this lady; it is easy to imagine her feelings in the face of an order so little expected. She nevertheless received it like a courageous lady; she is Japanese by birth, and this people is dauntless in the face of adversity. There are several examples of their facing death so resolutely that they approach insensitivity. With her son, she left the house where she had been lodged since her arrival in Bangkok; on her departure the Jesuit Fathers uttered some words of consolation. There were also some officers present, including Mr de La Salle, commissioner-general. She knew him by his reputation and his position; she charged him to relate to our king the treatment she had received, her being in possession of letters from this great monarch agreeing to take Mr Constance and his family into his protection. She paid her respects to the officers; she well realized by their expression that they had no part in this act; she was then handed over to the *painted arms*—this is the name given to the hangmen in Siam—and the consequences fill me with horror. Thus she left the fort without shedding a tear, proud in looks and gait, while the Frenchmen were grieved to see such a person in the hands of their enemies. The officers who had been arrested in Siam were released, and everyone prepared to leave. It was known that the Siamese were tenacious in retaining this lady for two reasons: one was that they still thought to discover through her where the late Mr Constance had hidden his wealth, the other reason was the continuing passion felt for her by Petracha's son. It is suspected that Mr Desfarges had some stake in being so firm in his resolve to hand the lady over. (III, 22–25)

This is Martin's description of perhaps the most disgraceful episode in a sordid adventure; his final comment, suspecting Desfarges of having a financial interest in the retention of Mme Phaulkon, is probably near the mark. There are indications that Phaulkon used Desfarges to carry some of the minister's wealth to France with him; if so, with Phaulkon dead and his wife safely out of the way, there would be no other claimants. It seems almost impossible to believe that Desfarges could be so despicable, but he is generally credited (not just by Martin, who was to know him personally) with being covetous. Challe is merciless in this respect, writing of Desfarges' "vulgar avarice, his unreasonable jealousy, his interested trust... Under his command the French...in spite of themselves were responsible for a thousand vile cowardices and lost in that kingdom the reputation of the French name." (1979: 510)

With Mme Phaulkon back in prison in Ayutthaya, the last obstacle to the French departure "with full honours" was removed. There were to be yet further examples of cowardice and broken promises.

The embarkation took place on 2 November 1688 one year to the day after the entry of the troops into Bangkok; several *miron*—this is the name given to their country boats—were loaded with cannons, munitions, and victuals; there were some Frenchmen guarding these boats. The bishop was in one to accompany Mr Desfarges to the mouth of the river, and Sieur Véret in another on the same pretext. There was great haste in going downstream: the three Siamese hostages were in the vessel carrying Mr Desfarges. Sieur Véret, who had decided his course of action, came up with his boat and also got on board. This departure was in some confusion, not to use a stronger term. The Siamese, noticing that the bar at the river mouth had been crossed, stopped the boats remaining behind. There were thirty iron cannons, victuals, and the French who had been placed on board as guards, but not in sufficient numbers to be able to force their passage. The bishop also remained behind; when the boats arrived in the roads and anchored with the other boats which followed, the Siamese demanded that the treaty be executed to the letter, with the return of their hostages and also Sieur Véret to remain in Siam. Mr Desfarges sought the boats which had been stopped and said he would send them [Véret and the hostages] when these arrived. There were loud protests. The bishop wrote to the general; he implored him to keep his word and to consider what the condition the Frenchmen who remained in Siam would be in if he broke it. Mr Desfarges only released one of the hostages and promised to hand over the other two if the bishop and the Frenchmen who were in the boats were allowed to come on board. This proposal, it could be anticipated, was one that the Siamese could not accept, because by sending off the prelate and Sieur Véret who had already embarked they would have no guarantor for the vessels they had supplied or the advances they had made for the purchase of victuals. After a few days of discussion during which nothing could be agreed, the Siamese limiting themselves to seeking the execution of the treaty, the vessels set sail, the *Oriflamme*, the *Louveau*, and a small boat called the *Vérette*. The Abbé de Lionne and ... [blank] Missionaries were also on board. Remaining in Siam were the bishop and a further ... [blank] Missionaries. The only Jesuit to remain there was Fr de Labreuille; the other Fathers had embarked. Also left behind were two officers, some soldiers, some merchants and some workmen. We shall return to them in our account.

The boats reached the open seas a few days later. On the announcement by Sieur Véret of the existence of a few islands nearby on which he claimed there were cloves and nutmegs, the ships dropped anchor. People spoke for and against; some said that they found nutmegs, but as they provided no proof and the reports could be suspect, they were not believed and there seemed in truth to be none. The monsoon then blowing towards the coast, the vessels passed the Straits of Malacca, and anchored a few days in front of this stronghold; they then set sail again from there and came to cast anchor before Pondichéry, as I have related. (III, 26–27)

This inglorious and duplicitous departure had Véret as well as Desfarges going back on their word. Small wonder that the Frenchmen who remained in Siam were to suffer considerably. But Desfarges then launched into a further idiocy.

CHAPTER ELEVEN

THE EXPEDITION TO PHUKET, 1689

ONCE in Pondichéry, Desfarges lost no time in trying to save what remained of his tattered reputation by embarking on a military expedition. His obstinacy in this, and possibly his self-interest, are more evident than his good sense. Only two days after the *Oriflamme* had arrived, he launched his latest proposal.

Mr Desfarges called a meeting of the council the 6th [February 1689]; the persons who constituted it were the general, Mr de Bruant, Mr de Vertesalle, Mr d'Estrille, captain of the *Oriflamme*, and Mr de La Salle, commissioner-general. I was also in the assembly, as well as Sieur J.-B. Martin, my deputy. Sieur Véret also took part, as did Sieur de La Mare, engineer. At issue was what to do with the vessels and the troops; at first there was question of going to the island of Junk Ceylon [Phuket]. Sieur Véret had spoken about this to Mr Desfarges who fully supported his views. The officers had no knowledge of this island; they followed the desires of the general who was much in favour of it. Sieur de La Mare, who knew something of it from a confused report, and who had been admitted to the assembly (though he was not there in the capacity of a voting member), to give incentive to the voyage, greatly exaggerated the utility, abundance, and wealth of Junk Ceylon. I was informed of the contrary, as was Sieur J.-B. Martin, by four or five journeys undertaken from Pondichéry in the interests of the Company; I spoke against this exaggeration entirely opposed to the truth. I also called in Sieur Germain who had been employed as captain of the vessels we had sent to this island, who publicly contradicted the engineer. He, though, still held fast to his view, supported by Sieur Véret. I could not understand the reasons which incited these two men to so futile a voyage; I spoke again and told Mr Desfarges that, if there was an enterprise to be undertaken in the Indies, it should be directed to Mergui, the best and the most advantageous for the Company, that we had sufficient forces to maintain ourselves there, it was only twelve or fifteen days at most from the [Coromandel] coast, and where it was possible to enter and leave at almost all seasons. This proposal did not please all the persons in the assembly; the discussion returned to Junk Ceylon. I then suggested that everyone give his reasons in writing; I received no support. Finally as everyone was in favour of the island of Junk Ceylon, one had to swim with the stream. A resolution was made in twelve or fifteen lines which the assembly signed. Measures were then taken to prepare the things necessary for the voyage; rice was bought, and other legumens for the crews and the soldiers. As we had no right to kill cows in Gentile lands [around Pondichéry], it was arranged with the Brahmins to buy buffaloes which were salted. People were despatched to Madras to buy rigging; the vessels were in poor condition, particularly the *Siam*; it was repaired as well as possible and as far as the facilities permitted in an open roadstead. (III, 27–8)

Desfarges continued his high-handed ways. In the night of 16 and 17 February, the *Normande* and the *Coche* left for France, with two Jesuits on boat, a packet of letters for the court from the general, and

Sieur de Sainte-Marie, he who had brought Mme Phaulkon from Siam to Bangkok and whom the general dismissed, as well as Sieur Vollant [des Verquins], engineer. Mr Desfarges charged the latter with not fulfilling his duties, though he had attestations to the contrary from other officers and it is also certain that passion entered into this dismissal. (III, 30)

Vollant des Verquins had, like de La Mare (with whom naturally he disagreed), drawn up numerous plans for Vaubanesque fortresses in Siam; he published two years later his account of the Siamese revolution. Martin does not say so, but one of the Jesuits was Fr Le Blanc, who published his account of events in 1692. The ships on which these persons were travelling were to go via the Cape of Good Hope with letters for the squadron commander expected from France, informing him of events in Siam, and ordering him to proceed to Pondichéry. Fate was not kind to them; by the time they arrived at the Cape, the Augsburg League was at war with France; both ships were seized by the Dutch, and the French were taken to Holland and imprisoned in Middelburg. Martin anticipates the relation of this event in his record of February (III, 30), and was partially able to confirm it in September: "Rumour for the past month has it that the two French boats were seized at the Cape. We finally had confirmation of this untoward news. It is really too distressful to dwell on, and a continuation of the ill-success of our Siamese venture." (III, 55)

Meanwhile, preparations for the expedition to Phuket continued.

Mr de l'Estrille, who normally stayed on board [his ship] the *Oriflamme*, came ashore to decide upon the day of departure of the vessels for Junk Ceylon. There were many officers who were not in favour of this voyage; apart from the scant utility to be drawn from this enterprise, they feared landing in unknown territory where they might well not find the means of survival. When a council was held, the persons who took part had to promise to reveal nothing of what was discussed, but the natural French propensity prevailed over this precaution. The purpose of the voyage was known throughout Pondichéry two hours after Mr de l'Estrille came ashore, and provoked objections. However, after many reasons for and against, it was decided to embark the troops the 26th and then to set sail. (III, 31)

Meanwhile problems continued with the English East India Company in Madras; a court had been set up to decide the fate of the prizes the *Mergui* and the *Lorette* (as noted in chapter eight, Martin had protested about the seizure of these ships which brought the remnants of the French from Mergui). The latter was adjudged to belong to the King of Siam and so was a legitimate prize; judgment on the *Mergui* was deferred (III, 31–2).

Trouble accumulated for Martin: Pondichéry was threatened with attack by the Indians, and he asked Desfarges for a company of soldiers to remain. Desfarges merely deferred the request, saying he would discuss it with de Bruant and de Vertesalle (III, 33).

L'Estrille wrote on 30 March to de La Salle, the commissioner-general, to warn Desfarges that the time taken to prepare the departure for Junk Ceylon had been exceeded, and it was necessary to decide what to do next. Martin says he had spoken about this with the general a few days previously, suggesting he wait for letters from France, which would certainly arrive via Surat in April, and that the *Oriflamme* and the other ships take to the open sea to avoid the bad weather which often arrived in April there. Desfarges could wait until May when the monsoon for Junk Ceylon would be stronger, and there would be no delay as long as no letters arrived. Surprisingly, Desfarges agreed. There followed a quadrille of niceties of rank involving the transmission of the decision through de Bruant, de La Salle, and de l'Estrille. The commander of the *Oriflamme* was for taking to the high seas. The commissioner-general then "made a proposal to Mr Desfarges which did not seem well conceived and which did not therefore please him." L'Estrille wanted two companies of soldiers to embark on his ship, and would go ahead to Junk Ceylon, with his troops and crew, seize the island which he would fortify while waiting for the general and the rest of the troops and ships; "he was thanked for his bravery and good intentions." (III, 34)

Martin was hoping that the ships would ride the high seas and the troops would remain in Pondichéry, but on 3 April there came a report from the officers of the *Siam* and the *Louveau*, the two Siamese ships on loan which had travelled with the French from Bangkok, that the vessels were in no condition to go to sea for long, and could only just reach Junk Ceylon. Other officers were dispatched to check and said the same thing. Martin detected some intrigue; some people wanted to remain, and fearing not finding in Junk Ceylon the wherewithal to repair the ships, wished to dissociate themselves from the expedition. Martin again spoke in favour of Mergui to Desfarges, pointing out that the condition of the ships was better suited for such an expedition. Junk Ceylon again carried the day though; de l'Estrille was told everyone would embark in four or five days and finally carry out the resolution taken on 6 February (III, 34–5).

Martin received news on 4 April that the Madras court had decided to hand over the *Mergui* to the French; he still sought restitution of the *Lorette* as the situation was the same. Of more immediate concern was the departure of the troops for Phuket.

Desfarges decided this would be on 6 April. The troops were assembled on a parade ground, marched along the shore and transported in small boats to the ships in the roads. To avoid desertions, officers were posted on the sides and at the rear of the batallion. Martin still sought some troops to remain for the defence of Pondichéry; de Bruant saw his need but objected to a diminution of troop strength; de Vertesalle was adamantly opposed. Desfarges overrode both and gave Martin a company and three officers.

Fearing that not enough provisions could be found on Junk Ceylon to feed the troops and the crews, Martin had written to his son-in-law Deslandes in Bengal to buy some and send them on the *Saint-Nicholas*; the ships in Pondichéry were also loaded with "an assortment of trade goods lacking in those parts" to sell and buy foodstuffs with the proceeds.

> Mr de l'Estrille went three leagues off on the 8th; Mr Cornuel, second officer of the *Oriflamme* and Sieur Daumont, ensign, were sent ashore to speed up the embarkation; this was complete on the 9th in the morning. The general was to travel on the *Oriflamme*, Mr de Bruant on the *Siam*, and Mr de Vertesalle on the *Louveau*, and the troops were dispersed among them according to the ships' size. The Jesuit Fr Thionville and the Missionary from Siam Mr Ferreux also went on board, and the two Siamese hostages were taken too. The two [smaller] vessels set sail at four in the morning on the 10th; at four in the afternoon we received letters from Surat. (III, 37)

With the departure of the Desfarges expedition for Phuket, Martin could concentrate on traditional trading. He had still to receive the *Mergui*, which was finally handed over in Madras on 1 May (it did not arrive in Pondichéry until the 18th). Pondichéry continued to receive sundry Missionaries and other clerics. The Jesuit Duchatz and two Missionaries from Siam, Joret and Genou, passed through en route for Pegu (III, 39). Also in May, the Abbé de Lionne, who had left Bangkok with the retreating French, went to Madras with another Missionary, Pin, accompanied by the Jesuits Fr de Bèze (to be a great source of information concerning events in Lopburi and Bangkok in 1688) and Fr Comilhe, to go from Madras to China (III, 41).

More letters came for Desfarges, de Bruant, and de La Salle on 31 May on the *Lonré* which had left Britanny in October 1688; there was also a partially sealed letter for "the Count Phaulkon". As war had broken out in Europe following the expulsion of James II by William of Orange, it was important to let Desfarges know. The ketch the *Saint-Joseph* was sent to Phuket on 6 June loaded with letters, "wine and other refreshments" (III, 43).

In October 1689 came a piece of news not found in other accounts of the consequences of the May 1688 *coup d'état*, showing the new *phra klang*, Kosa Pan, to be both decisive and diplomatic:

> Notice of an uprising occurring in Tenasserim reached us. The mandarin in command supported by the local people wanted to make himself sovereign; he raised troops and sought to advance his preparations. The new King of Siam [Petracha] acted in his turn to prevent this; the *barcalon* set out with twelve or fifteen thousand men armed according to the custom of the country. This general had the adroitness after his arrival in the province to win over the chief conspirators; the revolt weakened because of this, and the rest were soon dissipated. The guilty who were taken were punished with the usual tortures applied in that nation and thus tranquillity returned to the land. (III, 59)

The following month came letters from Deslandes in Bengal, indicating that the *Saint-Nicholas* had left with victuals for the troops in Phuket; soon after came news from Phuket itself, with the return of the *Saint-Joseph* on the 23rd to Pondichéry. Duval, the captain reported

> that he had been to Junk Ceylon where he had not found the [French] vessels, that he had found a local man who assured him that nothing had been seen of them, and that after leaving Junk Ceylon he went before the port of Mergui where he fired cannon shots as a signal to our people who might be there, but only three galleys came close to, and he did not think it prudent to wait for them, having only five Frenchmen on board. He then went to a port four leagues from the fortress, from where he could observe every movement in and out of Mergui, and where he remained two

and a half months. Finally, meeting no one, he decided to return. (III, 65–6)

Martin did not believe Duval, being certain that when he should have been in Phuket, the squadron was there; Martin was convinced Duval had never gone to Phuket at all.

It was not until 7 February 1690 that Martin received information of what had happened to Desfarges and his troops, when ships arriving from Balassor in Bengal brought news that the French had taken on victuals there. The *Oriflamme*, the *Lonré*, and the *Saint-Nicholas* all arrived in Pondichéry on 11th, and the following day the officers came ashore.

We learnt that after leaving Pondichéry for Junk Ceylon, the vessels dropped anchor at an island some twenty-five or thirty leagues from Junk Ceylon, which they baptized Colbert Island, and where they took on water and wood. It was noted that this island had very fine trees for making masts, suitable for the biggest ships in use in Europe. The vessels stayed there ten or eleven days, then set sail and anchored near Junk Ceylon. It is difficult to report the truth of the conduct observed in this voyage, given the diversity of the reports. Mr de Bruant assured me that no one had recognized Junk Ceylon, and they had gone to another island nearby and said I could even report this to France. Those disinterested and without partiality agreed that the ships anchored near to Junk Ceylon, but they also admitted that they did not recognize the island from the strait from which they should approach it, and where there is a wide bay (and, in the maps on which the voyage had been based has the appearance of a harbour), that the island was only recognized by the coast which is opposite; and after having sent people in longboats to go ashore, they found the whole place flooded, without habitation, and saw no one. On the report which they gave on their return, people were sick of the whole enterprise. Those who had so passionately advanced this voyage had nothing to say, except that they were ill-informed; meanwhile the vessels stayed at anchor waiting for orders which were promised them. The officers sought refreshments by hunting on neighbouring islands, where there was plenty of game; fish were also caught.

The small ship the *Vérette* under the command of Sieur Lemoyne, first lieutenant of the *Oriflamme*, was sent from there to go and cruise in the strait of ... [blank], and reconnoitre if French ships were passing for Siam, in order to inform the officers of the state of affairs in that kingdom. Sieur Lemoyne met a Portuguese boat going to ... [blank]; he learnt from the captain of the declaration of war in Europe. He also boarded a Chinese vessel transporting some Europeans who confirmed the news. He recognized from this that it was not prudent to stay in those parts and returned to Junk Ceylon where he transmitted the news. He was followed on his return by a Dutch vessel but managed to give it the slip.

During the voyage of this small boat, the *Saint-Nicholas* had arrived from Bengal with its cargo of victuals; it was a great relief for the crews who were in need of them.

Mr Desfarges called together a council on the news of war in Europe; everyone agreed that the squadron should return to Pondichéry, where they could take the necessary decisions according to the views and orders which they expected to find there. However, as it seemed most likely that they would be required to return to France, it was considered appropriate to go to Balassor and there take on victuals for the journey. The monsoon having not yet begun to reach there, it was decided to go and anchor in Negrais, on the coast of Pegu, whilst waiting for a favourable wind to continue the journey. These two decisions taken, they put ashore the two mandarins who had served as hostages for the treaty of Bangkok and who they had brought along. The Missionary Mr Ferreux, out of zeal and purely Christian charity, in order to assist the Bishop of Metellopolis and the other Missionaries who had been arrested, went voluntarily with the two mandarins to travel to Siam [Ayutthaya]. He had foreseen this course of action before leaving

Pondichéry, and took with him money to assist the Missionaries and the French who were imprisoned.

The vessels set sail from thence [Phuket] and went to drop anchor at Negrais. Whilst they stayed there, the crews and the troops regained their health marvellously; deer, boars, and buffaloes were hunted, and fishing yielded all kinds of fish. After this improving stay, the ships weighed anchor and then went to moor at Balassor. The intendant went up to Hougly where Mr Deslandes gave orders to assemble the victuals needed for a journey to France. The *Lonré* and the *Saint-Nicholas* belonging to the Company were also loaded, the first with local merchandise, the *Saint-Nicholas* with victuals for Pondichéry, and both for their return to France with the *Oriflamme*. Everything being ready for departure, Mr Desfarges left at Balassor the *Siam*, the *Louveau*, and the *Vérette*. These ships were not in a condition to make the journey; they were moored in the river, and the *Oriflamme*, the *Lonré*, and the *Saint-Nicholas* set sail for Pondichéry where they dropped anchor. (III, 77–80)

Once ashore, Desfarges and de Bruant asked Martin for his views on what should be done with the troops, since the letters brought by the *Lonré* did not specify, as nothing was known of the *coup d'état* in Siam before the ship had set sail from France. Martin replied that nothing could be done in the Indies given the war with the Dutch and apparently the English. The Company could not afford to support forty officers and more than 300 soldiers, many men would desert, the troops would be more useful in France, and the arrival of a French squadron in Pondichéry could not be counted on because of the war. Desfarges decided to return with his troops, "disheartened by their ill-success" and the discomfort they had endured. But de Bruant wanted to remain, and advanced all kinds of specious reasons for this; Martin learnt later that de Bruant was certain Desfarges would be recalled and he would be nominated to succeed him. Finally it was agreed on a return to France, leaving 108 soldiers in two companies, four officers, and three sergeants. The three ships set sail on 21 February 1690 for France. (III, 81–2)

Strictly nothing was gained from the expedition to Phuket; indeed, no one was sure that Phuket had even been reached. From his arrival in Pondichéry at the beginning of February 1689, to the much-delayed departure for Phuket on 10 April, and the return of the ships on 11 February 1690, a whole year had been wasted to no purpose. Instead of returning at once to Pondichéry once news of war in Europe had reached him, knowing how much in need of succour the French outpost was from possible attacks by the English and Dutch, Desfarges further dallied in the Bay of Bengal. Knowing his pecuniary interests, it seems likely that the stop in Balassor was contrived as much to acquire Indian trade goods as victuals for the return journey to France. Small wonder that Desfarges feared the rope on his return. Death came sooner than expected though, as will be seen in the final chapter.

CHAPTER TWELVE

THE DUQUESNE-GUITON SQUADRON, 1690–1

THE original purpose of sending the Duquesne-Guiton squadron to Southeast Asian waters was in support of French troops and interests in Siam, but the death of King Narai, the execution of Phaulkon, the accession of the usurper Petracha to the throne, and the war in Europe with the Grand Alliance, to last from 1689 to 1697, changed all that. Details concerning the squadron are beyond the scope of this book, except in so far as they touch on Siam, which the squadron never in fact reached; its entire voyage is marked by futility, for, give or take the odd prize seized, it achieved nothing, rather like Desfarges' expedition to Phuket. Readers interested in its peregrinations are referred to Robert Challe's contemporary account, *Journal d'un voyage fait aux Indes orientales (1691–1691)*.

Martin first received news of the departure of the squadron on 11 August 1690, five months after it had already left Brittany, bearing among others the intriguing Fr Tachard and three attendant Siamese mandarins, returning from the Jesuit's mission as King Narai's representative to Pope Innocent XI and Louis XIV. Martin learnt that the six vessels comprising the small fleet (the *Gaillard*, the *Oiseau*, the *Florissant*, the *Ecueil*, and two small frigates, the *Lion* and the *Dragon*), all commanded by Duquesne-Guiton, had left Port-Louis and gone first to the Cape Verde Islands, had seized an English ship near the Comoros, taken a heavily-laden Dutch vessel off Ceylon, and then set sail for Pondichéry. The whole squadron arrived in the roads the following day (III, 105–8).

Duquesne came ashore on the 13th bringing the usual packets of letters; the vessels were to be loaded with trade goods in the Company's warehouses, then go to Bengal, and either return to Pondichéry or go straight from Balassor to France (III, 108).

We learnt from Mr Duquesne that last year five vessels were ready to leave for the Indies. When information reached France of the revolutions which had occurred in Siam, their departure was delayed. The Marquis de Ragny [d'Eragny] was to have been on board, as inspector and captain of the palace guard, [comprising] young men specially selected for the King of Siam; there were also orders for me to go to Mergui, where we were to apply ourselves to the construction of a strong fortress; the council would have consisted of Mr Desfarges, the Marquis de Ragny, Mr de Bruant, and me. There were also orders for Mr Deslandes to go to Siam from where the Company would withdraw Sieur Véret. All these arrangements were changed by the events I have related. Given the doubt that obtained in France at the time of departure of the squadron whether the troops remained in the Indies, in the case the squadron met with them, there were orders that if there seemed to be the likelihood of establishing a good outpost in the Indies, Mr de Bruant should remain as commander in place of Mr Desfarges, who was to return to France. These last orders were nullified by the return of the officers and troops [to France].

The Rev. Fr Tachard was on one of the ships with two other Jesuit priests, four brothers of the same order, some Siamese who were being sent back from France, two Tonkinese, and other persons. Fr Tachard had returned to the Indies to see if there was the possibility of re-establishing relations with Siam; he bore a letter from the pope, written by the Holy Father to the late King of Siam in reply to another letter and presents which this monarch had sent him, which had obliged Fr Tachard to go to Rome. His Reverence was also charged with a letter from our king to the late King of Siam.

There was another important matter which brought the Rev. Fr on this journey, concerning the differences which had arisen in Tonkin and China between the French Jesuits and the bishops and Missionaries of the Foreign Missions of the *Propaganda fidei*. A kind of agreement had been reached in Paris by order of the king, and in which the archbishop had acted as intermediary between the Jesuits and the Missionaries. Mr Charmot, one of the latter, had also come with the squadron in order, conjointly with Fr Tachard, to ensure the application of this agreement in the Indies by both sides. (III, 108-9)

This is the same Charmot we met in chapter five, and misfortune continued to dog him: his cabin was almost blown to pieces in one engagement, whilst that of Tachard unfairly remained unscathed.

Whilst the French fleet prepared to attack the Dutch ships in Madras, Tachard and Charmot went on board the squadron in the hope of reaching Mergui with the vessels; Tachard only took with him the Siamese who were to return to their country (III, 113). The squadron duly attacked, and finally returned to Pondichéry via Balassor on 12 January 1691, bringing news of its subsequent exploits in Bengal and Negrais, where some hundred men died of various illnesses (as Martin remarks, in contrast with what happened to the remnants of troops from Siam under Mr Desfarges, who had greatly improved their health there after their voyage to Junk Ceylon). Tachard and Charmot had not been able to land in Mergui, since Duquesne "did not find it appropriate to undertake the voyage" (III, 137).

The nearest the squadron got to Siam were some uninhabited islands to the north of Mergui, though the Siamese mandarins accompanying Fr Tachard were supposed to be landed in this port. One reason for not going into the port was undoubtedly that the

French were still uncertain of the reception that they would be given in 1690, so soon after the seige of their fort in Bangkok in 1688 and their breach of the treaty covering their withdrawal, not to mention the expedition to Phuket the previous year. Another reason was that the ships were not in a condition to engage in combat if required; more than one hundred men were lost while spending almost four weeks off Negrais (Smithies 1993: 92). The weather too was an obstacle: Challe (1979: 326) records there was not a breath of wind and "the devil protects the Siamese idols and does not want us to lay hands on them."

Tachard's two remaining Siamese mandarins (Ok-khun Chamnan and Ok-khun Wiset; a third, Ok-muen Pipith, like his colleagues one of the first Siamese officials known to have converted to Catholicism, had the misfortune to die early during the return voyage) were eventually offloaded at Balassor to return to Mergui by whatever means offered (III, 137). The squadron took on board what trade goods remained in the stores, and the loaded squadron set sail during the night of 23 January.

There remained some loose ends, not so much attached to the Duquesne-Guiton squadron, as to the ships plying the waters of the Bay of Bengal. The situation at Pondichéry was uncertain; it was ill-prepared to resist attack, and the Dutch were preparing an offensive. Martin sent off all unnecessary personnel, though Tachard remained, along with other Jesuits and the procurer of the Foreign Missions, Mr de La Vigne (III, 141).

The Siamese vessels taken from Bangkok, the *Siam* and the *Louveau*, and the *Mergui* seized in the withdrawal from Mergui, had not been returned. The first two had arrived in Pondichéry on 1 February 1689. Both had finally gone on the useless expedition to Phuket, and had been abandoned at Balassor. In May 1691 Martin noted that, like the *Aigle*, the *Siam* and the *Louveau* had been placed in dock in Balassor in an attempt to preserve them (III, 150). He wrote at the same time:

> Those things which had been made in France for the late King of Siam had been loaded in the squadron of six vessels in order to try and sell them in the Indies and had been offloaded in Bengal. They were not found to be appropriate for that region, nor wherever they were sent, and it was necessary to return them to the factory; it was a useless stock which remained in the stores without being able to extract any profit from it and which was deteriorating over time. (III, 150)

Challe in December 1690 saw the *Siam* at Balassor; it was "bigger, stronger, and more beautiful than any in our squadron...they dare not put it to sea, fearing an incident. It is certainly a pity that such a fine vessel remains unused and decaying." (1979: 374) There it stayed.

More news concerning the Siamese ships came in January 1692: "The King of Siam [Petracha] had written to the viceroy of Bengal to demand the *Siam* and the *Louveau* which remained in the river and which he maintained were his; nothing had been determined up to then about this matter." (III,182) Martin supplies no further information about the vessels. They probably deteriorated to such as extent that they were useless; in January 1693 Martin noted that the *Mergui*, still in Bengal, was in such a bad condition that Deslandes sold it to a Portuguese merchant for 4,450 rupees (III, 272). The *Aigle* was sold at the same time to Armenian merchants, after "withdrawing the cast-iron cannons with which this vessel had been armed in Siam, when Mr Céberet was dealing with Mr Constance." (III, 272) How long ago all that seemed by then!

The Duquesne-Guiton expedition is of little direct concern in an assessment of Franco-Siamese relations; Challe's account of it, though, contains numerous references to Siam, to persons involved in the events of 1688, and not least to Tachard, whom he clearly loathed (a sentiment shared by many). His account also contains a lengthy "conference with Mr Martin", purporting to be the expression of Martin's views to Challe, given in Pondichéry on 25 January 1691. Challe details Tachard's involvement in trading and diamond smuggling, which "is directly contrary to the precepts of Jesus Christ concerning missions" (1979: 422). The Jesuits, in words purported to come from François Martin, "are hated as the very devil, and yet respected by everyone because everyone fears them." (1979: 443)

The expedition was in many respects the final loose end as far as formal French contacts with Siam were concerned; Tachard, as will be seen, was given carte blanche to do what he liked with his letters to the now-dead King Narai, and was clearly considered by Versailles an embarrassing irrelevance in the changed political circumstances. But there remained a number of other loose ends, not least the fate of those who had been left behind in Siam and Pegu.

CHAPTER THIRTEEN

THE AFTERMATH, 1688–93

THE FRENCH IN AYUTTHAYA

Desfarges had little thought of the treatment the Frenchmen remaining in Ayutthaya were likely to receive in the hands of the Siamese, justly furious at the breaking of nearly every clause in the treaty negotiated for the French retreat from Bangkok.

In June 1689 news came from Siam in letters addressed by the Bishop of Metellopolis to Fr de La Vigne, procurer-general for the Foreign Missions who was in Pondichéry. Martin writes:

> There was nothing more touching than the misery to which this illustrious prelate, the Missionaires, Fr Labreuille, and all the French who were in those parts were reduced after the departure of Mr Desfarges. After all the ill-use in which the most barbarous people can inflict on persons of merit and distinction, the bishop was imprisoned in a bamboo hovel covered with straw or leaves, the Jesuit, the Missionaries and the other Frenchmen were dispersed in common prisons, mixed with criminals and the greatest rogues, the cagne round their necks, their feet and hands in the stocks. Thus they passed their nights. In the morning, the French were taken out, chained to criminals, and taken to work, carrying bricks, earth or employed in other occupations which it was considered appropriate

129

for them, their tormentors escorting them to advance the work, and not a grain of rice for their food. The Siamese had left two Missionaries free to supply the prisoners with food; some goods which they had fortunately hidden and had not been discovered, and the charity they received, even from Manila, served to sustain our people. One could write several volumes about the distress they suffered. The Dutch refused to lend money to the bishop; he spoke of this to the head of their factory, and provided sound guarantees to repay them. The inhumanity of this refusal was evident particularly in respect of a prelate whose merit and character should inspire all honest people to particular distinction. (III, 45-6)

Martin is being a little naive here; the French had shown no mercy to their own Protestants after the revocation of the Edict of Nantes in 1685, and there was no reason why the Protestant Dutch should give any assistance to the French Catholics in Siam, especially since they had broken their treaty agreement with the Siamese. In terms of practical politics, too, the Dutch saw no reason to succour the pariahs of the day.

Martin recorded no further news of the mission in Siam for another year. In June 1690 he noted:

Letters came from Aceh saying that since the return of the two hostages who had been landed on the island of Junk Ceylon, and the arrival of Mr Ferreux, the bishop and the gentlemen Missionaries had been allowed more liberty, and the other Frenchmen were exempt from the daily tasks they had been given, but were still held prisoner and in irons. (III, 94)

As seen in chapter eleven, Ferreux had decided to accompany the two Siamese mandarins to Ayutthaya and give what assistance he could to the Mission. It is not known precisely when the three were put ashore in Phuket, but was probably at the end of 1689.

In July 1690 Martin received letters from the Bishop of Metellopolis himself, containing an account of

> a succession of afflictions to which this prelate and the gentlemen Missionaries and other Frenchmen had been reduced by the treatment they suffered in the prisons where they still languished in irons; they were only exempted from hard labour since the return to Siam of the two hostages and Mr Ferreux. (III, 103)

More letters came in February 1691 from Louis Laneau, Bishop of Metellopolis:

> this great prelate informed us that the Missionaries were freed and allowed to go about the town; the other Frenchmen were still locked up in prison. Some Missionaries and some other Frenchmen had died from the afflictions and the ill-treatment they had suffered. (III, 142)

Things were getting better, but very slowly. In April 1691 further letters from Siam arrived, with no change in the condition of those imprisoned (III, 148). In June 1691 came more letters from the bishop, indicating still no change, but with one additional piece of information: "The news that reached the court of the arrival of our squadron [commanded by Duquesne-Guiton] off the coasts had raised the alarm. The bishop gave to understand that their lives were at risk if there was the least attack on the territory of the kingdom." (III, 153)

There follows a curious paragraph in Martin's memoirs: "There was an uprising in Padang; the *barcalon* had left Siam [Ayutthaya] at the head of ten or twelve thousand men to return the people in that province to their duty." (III, 153) The source of this information is not given, but it immediately follows the passage on the latest letters received from the French bishop in Siam, who may or may not have supplied the news, which clearly relates to Siam, given the mention of the city and the *phra klang ('barcalon')*, at the time Kosa Pan, the former Siamese chief ambassador to Louis XIV. But there was no such province in Siam called Padang, which is situated in west Sumatra. One wonders if Martin might be referring to Pahang, or possibly Phatthalung, both among several southern centres occasionally in revolt against central authority.

The situation for the bishop, the Missionaries, and the incarcerated Frenchmen in Ayutthaya had eased considerably by February 1691, as will be seen below, and by July 1691 more encouraging news was received from Ayutthaya:

> We were informed in letters from Siam that if we wrote to the crown prince [Sorasak], the son of the king now reigning, and to the *barcalon*, we would easily obtain the release of the Frenchmen still held in the prisons. It was added that the court feared the return of our country to the kingdom, and it was well disposed to discuss a compromise. We thought it advisable to act on this information to try and secure the release of our Frenchmen from their plight and commit the Siamese to making some proposals. We wrote to the prince and the *barcalon*. Fr Tachard also wrote to them; the letters were sent in a small Moorish [Muslim] boat leaving for Manila, with 300 pieces of eight to help our king's officers, soldiers, and the Company's men in Siam. Mr de La Vigne, the procurer-general of the Foreign Missions, also sent by the same means 1,000 pieces of eight to be passed to the Bishop of Metellopolis, this means appearing safe, having succeeded for other transfers to the Mission. (III, 156)

The last news recorded by Martin of the position of the Missionairies and other Frenchmen in Ayutthaya arrived in March 1693:

> All the French were freed and the court of Siam was disposed to renew relations with our nation; it was even stated that it desired

them. The bishop had some difficulty in recovering from his ordeal in prison. Three or four Missionaries and several other Frenchmen had died, not having been able to recover their health. The Jesuit Fr Labreuille had withdrawn to the seminary, the Portuguese Jesuits not having been able to tolerate him among them. (III, 304)

Martin then explains the background to the spiritual division of the world by Pope Alexander VI between Spain and Portugal, and mentions the role of the Foreign Missions in propagating the gospels in various kingdoms, including Siam (III, 304–5). The saintly Louis Laneau, Bishop of Metellopolis, who had endured so much for his faith and his country, died in Ayutthaya in March 1696, aged fifty-nine, worn out by adversity and at the end of his life having to defend himself to the pope against the accusations of Portuguese Jesuits in Ayutthaya. The Mission which he had headed just managed to survive throughout the following century, but made few converts and was constantly short of funds.

BUCANEERS IN AYUTTHAYA

Martin relates one curious incident in February 1691 which tends to show that Petracha's wrath was not directed at the entire French nation, but only to those who had broken the treaty governing the retreat from Bangkok.

There arrived at Siam [Ayutthaya] a small boat with some Frenchmen on board. There were bucaneers from America who had passed the French islands [the Antilles] of the Southern Ocean through the Strait of Magellan, and, after several privateering trips and extortions off the coast of Peru and New Spain [Mexico], ten or twelve of them had taken possession of the prizes and with a small boat had arrived, after many adventures in Cochinchina and from there to Siam; they were well received there, and the King of Siam [Petracha] ordered that all the French who came to trade should be treated likewise. (III, 142)

More than two years later, in March 1693, two of these characters resurfaced in Pondichéry, having travelled from Mergui to Aceh and then to the French outpost. Martin says nothing further about them or their reception in Siam, except that they came bearing letters from the Bishop of Metellopolis, the Missionaries, and some French officers in Siam, as noted above (III, 303–4).

How long they stayed in Siam is not known, but clearly they were not hounded out of the country, even though their background was less than pristine.

TACHARD, PINEIRO, AND PETRACHA

Martin's letters written in July 1691 to Sorasak and Kosa Pan seemed to have had their effect, for in January 1692 he noted:

> We received notice on the 4th of this month of the arrival of an Armenian ship in Madras which came from Siam, on which were an envoy of the king with other Frenchmen and orders to proceed to Pondichéry. He was the bearer of letters from the *barcalon* and several packets for Fr Tachard, for the gentlemen of the Foreign Missions, and for us ... The envoy was a V. Pinheiro, a native of Siam but a Christian, who had been interpreter for the gentlemen of the Mission and then of the Company; the King of Siam had raised him to the rank of ... [blank: Ok-luang Worowathi] to validate his mission; [he had] two mandarins as deputies and some valets. He has been sent on the return to Siam by the persons of that nation whom Fr Tachard had left in Bengal and who had afterwards returned from there. These persons had been given a letter for the *barcalon*, which the Rev. Fr had written, in which he noted that he was charged with a letter from the Holy Father the Pope for the late king [Narai], and another from our king for the same monarch, that they had been written before his death was known, that he had kept them to present to the king now reigning when the occasion arose and it was safe to travel to Siam. The Rev.

Fr expatiated on general matters but it is not necessary to relate them here. The envoys were charged with the *barcalon*'s reply for His Reverence; it was carried cermoniously on the 22nd into their house. It began by acknowledging receipt of the Father's letter, then discussed the conduct of the late Mr Constance and the ill-use he had made of crown property, from there to the conduct of the French after the death of the late king, the lack of compliance with the treaty [of capitulation], the gentle handling he claimed to have given the French who stayed in Siam after the departure of Mr Desfarges, who were guilty of death according to the laws of the kingdom for having broken their general's word. All these facts were presented with skill, and those who knew nothing of the revolutions in Siam, of its consequences, and the cruelty of that people, would have been beguiled by it. The *barcalon* then discussed the situation in the kingdom, which did not fear the French, and the king was even ready to renew the contacts between the two countries, if France wished it, by re-establishing trade and religious links, according to the treaties drawn up under the late king. Fr Tachard was then invited to travel to Siam with the letters he was bearing, and [given] assurances that they would be received with the honour they were due, assured of the safety of his person and the Company's men who would travel with him to liquidate the account which existed with the king's stores (adding that V. Pinheiro and the other mandarins had been sent to accompany them). These were the chief matters in the *barcalon*'s letter. I opened one written to Mr Deslandes whom he knew well from his stay in Siam and who had written to him from Bengal at the same time as Fr Tachard when he was there. It was a kind of account of what had occurred in the revolutions, but phrased in such a way as to favour the Siamese, and one would have been persuaded by it if one did not know all that was contrary.

We learned by private letters that the bishop and the Missionaries had been re-established in their seminary, that the other Frenchmen had been released from the prisons in February 1691 and lodged in a private house, and that after the return to Siam of the Siamese from Bengal and notice of the arrival of the squadron, they too were free to withdraw to the seminary or go about town, but vouched for by the bishop, who had guaranteed to be responsible for anyone who absconded.

We were advised to have confidence in V. Pinheiro, who was zealous for our nation and could greatly help in arranging a settlement. Nothing could be said for certain concerning the feelings of the *barcalon* in regard to us. Some believed him well intentioned towards us, but that he feared to show this; others believed him our enemy, though he had greatly contributed to freeing the Frenchmen detained.

The kingdom of Siam was fairly peaceful at present. There were no further uprisings. The king was very disagreeable; he had a son by his wife, the daughter of the late king, and his eldest son by an earlier wife meddled greatly in the government. We were advised to write to him but above all not to speak of Bangkok or Mergui, only to limit ourselves to the treaties concerning religion and commerce.

Letters indicated that the Dutch were no longer so well favoured at [the Siamese] court, that they were held accountable for breaking their word in relation to promises given to the king, none of which they had fulfilled, though their trading continued well as before.

No positive replies were given at that time to V. Pinheiro and the mandarins. They were merely informed that we were entirely prepared to re-establish communication with them, being persuaded that the King of Siam would rule justly in respect of all French claims, that we were waiting for vessels and orders from France, that it was not appropriate for Fr Tachard and the persons accompanying him to embark on a foreign vessel, apart from there being no guarantee of safety for them. Vincent Pinheiro and his companions were lodged in the house of a Frenchman resident [in Pondichéry] and orders were given to provide them with all necessities. (III, 184–7)

Martin provides here valuable glimpses of events and personalities in Ayutthaya in these comments. Through him we receive confirmation that Princess Yothathep, King Narai's only child, was indeed forced to marry Petracha and had a son by him, thus legitimizing the usurpation. Confirmation is also provided of Petracha's irascible temper (which was to lead to the downfall of Kosa Pan). Confirmation too comes of Sorasak's considerable influence at court. Vicente Pinheiro, whose Siamese title was Ok-luang Worowathi, was of partly Portuguese origin. He reappears in Martin's memoirs a little later.

Two months after the arrival of Pinheiro in Pondichéry, in March 1692, Martin learnt that a small vessel was being prepared in Madras for the journey to Tenasserim, and it was decided to write to Siam what can only be termed temporizing letters.

> Fr Tachard replied to the *barcalon*, assuring him of his passage to Siam after the arrival of French ships which were expected, and of the disposition in which we were to renew relations between the two nations, hoping that the King of Siam was of the same inclination. I wrote, certain that the letters would be taken to the court first and that they would have to be interpreted; in them I dwelt on the need for the Siamese to consider their conduct towards the French and the advantages which would accrue to them by re-establishing our nation in their kingdom, but they ought to fear our king's resentment, and, to prove they were acting in good faith, to free the Frenchmen who remained in Siam and let them live with their compatriots. Mr de La Vigne, procurer-general of the Missions, also wrote and V. Pinheiro and his mandarins expatiated themselves as is their custom in their letters. They are rather like diaries in which they relate the smallest incidents. (III, 192–3)

This last fact struck all who met the Siamese ambassadors in France in 1686 (their secretaries went so far as to count the trees in the park at Saint-Cloud). Pinheiro became tired of waiting in Pondichéry, and decided to try and return to Siam via Madras. Martin wrote in September 1692:

Vincent Pinheiro, envoy of the King of Siam, about whom I spoke at length in February [in fact, January] this year, not seeing any Company ships arrive, and also not seeing the likelihood of any arriving, as the season was already ending, and the monsoon pressing for his return to Siam, decided in concert with the mandarins in his company to travel to Madras, and from there to Masulipatam, where he was informed there were ships taking on cargo for Mergui. He was given several letters for the crown prince, the king's son, for the *barcalon*, the Bishop of Metellopolis, the Missionaires and the French officers who were in that kingdom. It was realized that Pinheiro would be obliged to hand over to the *barcalon* all these letters, and that this official would have them examined. Care was taken to couch them in terms which would not jeopardize the bishop. It was also made clear that, providing the King of Siam gave the satisfaction expected of his justice, he would find France disposed to renew good relations between the two nations. He left on the 12th for Madras, but returned on the 28th, having found no means to travel by sea to Masulipatam, and there being too much danger in travelling overland because of brigands. (III, 243)

This is the last entry for Pinheiro in Martin's memoirs. The Siamese envoy remained in Pondichéry from January 1692 to May 1693, when he returned to Ayutthaya with a letter from Tachard seeking firmer guarantees from the *barcalon*. He was to play some role in the fraught negotiations leading up to the Jesuit's final appearance at court on 29 January 1699 (Vongsuravatana 1992: 314).

Meanwhile Fr Tachard stayed on in Pondichéry, only to be taken prisoner when the Dutch captured the French outpost in September 1693, when he was taken to Batavia and confined to an offshore island. Martin, a prisoner too but in better circumstances, pleaded for Tachard's release to go to China, but was told by the Dutch governor-general that "there were enough Jesuit Fathers in that empire" (III, 375). Instead, he was sent to Holland, where he arrived in July 1694, and allowed to go to Dunkirk, from where he reached Paris. He left again for the Indies in March 1695 with another French squadron, and reached Bengal in January 1697, sending yet another letter to the *barcalon*, hoping to return to Siam. He got as far as Mergui in February 1687, where he learnt the *barcalon* would not receive him in Ayutthaya (the excuse being that he had arrived on a merchant ship). After returning to Chandernagor, and nothing if not tenacious, accompanied by Fr Labreuille, he travelled on a French ship, the *Castricum*, from Balassor to Mergui, which he reached in October 1698, and finally arrived in Ayutthaya in January 1699. He spent three weeks in the capital, had at last his audience with Petracha, called on Mme Phaulkon, still a prisoner, slipping her some money, and left for Mergui, carrying a letter full of empty compliments for Louis XIV. He arrived in France in May 1700, presented his letter at Versailles, and returned for his fifth journey to the East; he arrived in Pondichéry in 1702, which he was forced to leave after conflicts with the governor who replaced Martin after his death in 1706, and died in Chandernagor, Bengal, on 21 October 1712.

King Petracha the usurper died in 1703; his son and heir apparent Sorasak (also known as Sua) became king, dying in 1709, to be succeeded likewise by his son. Problems of the succession, which had so bedevilled the end of King Narai's reign, were forgotten; Petracha's grandson, Phuminthararatcha (Thai Sa), reigned peacefully for twenty-four years.

THE FRENCH ABANDONED IN PEGU

The fate of the six Frenchmen abandoned in Pegu by de Bruant after the retreat from Mergui, related in chapter eight, was not a happy one. Martin received news of them in April 1689 in letters from a private merchant based in Pegu.

The Rev. Fr d'Espagnac, Sieur de Beauregard, and the other [four] Frenchmen who had been arrested during the voyage of Mr de Bruant in the bay had been condemned to death as enemies of the state, accused of sending vessels from Mergui to conduct a raiding expedition against the subjects of the King of Ava to whom Pegu is vassal, and of having taken and assaulted some of them. They managed however to find some people who affirmed they were Frenchmen who were withdrawing from Siam after a declaration of war by the natives against their nation, that they had no ill intention and had nothing to do with what had been undertaken against the Kingdom of Pegu, and that they had come to seek victuals which they lacked and which they would pay for; this was their only crime. It would seem that the Council which condemned them paid attention to those who represented them, and mollified its stance, the death sentence being commuted to perpetual slavery. They were then separated and sent inland, far from each other, without being able to communicate with each other except by some letters which they attempted to send when they found the occasion to give each other their news. The private merchant wrote suggesting that they could be released by sending an envoy and presents to the King of Ava. (III, 35–6)

Nothing seems to have come of this suggestion though, which arrived when Desfarges was still in Pondichéry before the departure of the expedition for Phuket; he was perhaps too concerned about possible gain there to worry about paying a ransom for his men in Pegu.

Just over a year later, Martin had further news (in May 1690) of those abandoned in Pegu by de Bruant, through "Fr Duchats". Jacques Duchatz was one of the fifteen Jesuits brought by Tachard (along with Claude de Bèze, Marcel Le Blanc, and Pierre d'Espagnac) to Siam with the La Loubère-Céberet mission. He was returning from Pegu, obviously having been there trying to secure the release of his fellow Jesuit.

He had been recognized in Ava by a Siamese interpreter who had seen the Father in Siam; the interpreter gave the mandarins to understand that he was one of the French who had tried to seize the kingdom and who were the cause of the disorders which arose there. The king was informed; this monarch then gave orders that he leave the city within twenty-four hours, be transported without delay to Syriam where he would be put on ship to remove him from the country, which orders were carried out. The Father then went to Madras on a Portuguese boat and from there to the fort [of Pondichéry]. Fr d'Espagnac, Sieur de Beauregard, and some other Frenchmen, those who had been arrested when Mr de Bruant passed by Tobay [Tavoy], were all inland, separated from each other, and very badly treated; a few had died in their misery. (III, 92)

In March 1692 Martin received confirmation of what was to be feared:

We received letters from Pegu concerning the death of the Jesuit Fr d'Espagnac, and that of Sieur de Beauregard; some time had elapsed since news of them last arrived, but it was not confirmed. Now there can be no further doubt. They had succumbed to the destitution to which they were reduced. Confirmed news of the other Frenchmen in their party had not been received. (III, 198)

Since some of the four accompanying them were already reported dead two years earlier, those who still remained alive almost certainly followed them to the grave soon after.

DESFARGES AND HIS MEN

Martin in February 1692 received letters relating the safe arrival in France of the *Lonré* and the *Saint-Nicholas*, which had left Pondichéry in February 1690 with the *Oriflamme*. The ships had been forced by adverse winds to go via Brazil where many persons died, as during the crossing up to then; from there to Martinique, Mr Desfarges, the Intendant, Mr Cornuel, second officer on the *Oriflamme*, the first lieutenant [all died], and, after their arrival in Martinique, Mr de l'Estrille, several officers, many soldiers, and crew members. The three vessels had set sail from there...but there was no news of the *Oriflamme* which was believed totally lost. (III, 191–2)

Still without news of the ship in June 1692, all hope for it was abandoned (III, 210); the *Oriflamme* is believed to have been struck by a fierce storm when approaching the coasts of Britanny, and to have sunk without trace on 27 February 1691. Desfarges was perhaps lucky to have died at sea, given the reception he is likely to have faced in France. His considerable fortune acquired in Siam, including sums handed over for safe-keeping by Phaulkon, passed to his two sons travelling on the same ship, the Marquis and the Chevalier Desfarges, who spent freely on their pleasures while in Martinique. They too did not live long to enjoy this wealth; they perished with the *Oriflamme*.

KOSA PAN

Kosa Pan, Ok-phra Wisut Sunthorn, chief ambassador to Louis XIV in 1686–7 and then *phra klang (barcalon)* after the *coup* of May 1688, appears from Martin's memoirs to have been a vigorous person, conducting negotiations with the French and leading expeditions against internal uprisings. After a typically angry outburst from Petracha, who cut off the end of his nose with a sword in 1696, he appears to have fallen in disgrace; his family were seized and tortured, and his possessions confiscated a few days before his death about June 1700, said to have been self-inflicted. According to the same Missionary relating these events, Braud, his body was not burnt but buried at night without honours (Launay 1920: 189).

COUNTESS PHAULKON

After the return of Mme Constance (Maria Guyomar de Pinha, also known as Dame Marie Guimard), Phaulkon's widow, and her surviving son George, to her Siamese captors on 18 October 1688 by Desfarges, she was condemned to perpetual slavery which was rigorously maintained until the death of Petracha in 1703 (van der Cruysse 1991: 469). According to a letter written in November 1688 by the Jesuit Maldonado to Louis XIV's confessor Fr de la Chaize, Mme Constance, her mother, aunts, and grandmother were "cast into the princesses's kitchens." (Ibid.) She apparently managed to resist the advances of Sorasak, Petracha's son and successor. Tachard saw her, still a slave in 1699 on his last, futile, visit to Siam. According to Reiko Hada (1992: 73) "She spent the rest of her life quietly in the Palace, teaching Siamese women how to make Portuguese and Japanese-style cakes, and supervising the missionary school she founded."

Her son George was raised in the French Seminary, and married locally a person of Portuguese descent; his son Constantine was in the service of King Borommakot (r.1733–1758) and is recorded as seeking persons capable of building a German organ for his master (Jacq-Hergoualc'h 1993: 111–2).

A petition was addressed to Louis XV (his great-grandfather, Louis XIV, having died in 1715) by "doña Guyomar de Piña, widow of Constance Phaulkon, and by Luisa Passana, widow of George Phaulkon, son of the former Siamese minister, claiming from the [French] Indies Company the liquidation of sums formerly provided by Constance, the restitution of capital disbursed and unpaid interest" (Lanier 1883: 196). A long legal battle ensued, the directors of the Company maintaining that the minister's widow had returned to favour in the court, the widow of his son had remarried a rich Irishman, and so both were not in need; that Phaulkon had not carried out his contractual agreements, having only provided half the promised sum; that his heirs, not having shared the Company's expenses and losses, were not due any recompense; and indeed the Company was owed sums by them, etc. The Council of State did not support their view, and on 26 June 1717 decreed both widows should be treated like all other Company creditors in connection of interest on sums paid in, and Phaulkon's widow should receive a pension of 3,000 *livres*.

It was a year later that Alexander Hamilton, spending some time in Ayutthaya in 1718, recorded meeting "my lady Phaulkon":

> she was then honoured with the superintendancy of His Majesty's confectionery. She was born in Siam of honourable parents, and at that time much respected both in the court and city for her prudence and humanity to nations and strangers when they came into difficulties or under the weight of oppression from the officers of the court or city. (Hamilton 1997: 167)

For all she herself had suffered at the hands of such officials, the Countess Phaulkon could indeed sympathize with those oppressed.

AND FRANÇOIS MARTIN?

Martin, the faithful Company servant, honest, prudent, and illegitimate, received letters in March 1692 conferring "patents of nobility which the king had had the goodness to grant me." (III, 258) But Pondichéry could hardly be defended, and the outpost capitulated to the Dutch on 7 September 1693. All the French were taken prisoner; some were sent to Ceylon, and some, including Martin, his wife, and Fr Tachard to Batavia (III, 366). In Batavia, where he arrived on 6 November, Martin was well received, but Tachard, as noted above, was not allowed to land (III, 371). The wife of the Dutch governor-general showed Martin and his wife the town, and on 13 November they left to go to Chandernagor in Bengal, passing close to Junk Ceylon, which had caused him so much trouble, on 7 January 1694 (III, 388). In Bengal in February 1694, where his son-in-law Deslandes continued as head of the French factory, Martin stopped writing his memoirs. He returned to Pondichéry in 1699, where he died on the last day of 1706. The ubiquitous Fr Tachard gave his funeral oration.

SELECT BIBLIOGRAPHY

BOURGES, Jacques de. *Relation du Voyage de Mgr l'Evêque de Béryte, Vicaire Apostolique du Royaume de la Cochinchine, par la Turquie, la Perse, les Indes, etc., jusqu'au Royaume de Siam et autres lieux.* Paris: Bechet, 1666.

BOUVET, Joachim. *Voyage de Siam.* Edited by J.C. Gatty. Leiden: Brill, 1963.

BRUMMELHUIS, Han ten. *Merchant, Courtier, and Diplomat: A History of the Contacts between the Netherlands and Thailand.* Lochem-Gent: Uitgeversmaatschappij de Tijdstroom, 1987.

CHALLE, Robert. *Journal d'un voyage fait aux Indes Orientales (1690–1691).* Edited by Frédéric Deloffre and Melâhat Menemencioglu. Paris: Mercure de France, 1979.

CHAUMONT, Chevalier de, and Abbé de CHOISY. *Aspects of the French Embassy to Siam, 1685.* Edited and in part translated by Michael Smithies. Chiang Mai: Silkworm Books, 1998.

CHOISY, Abbé de. *Journal of a Voyage to Siam 1685–1686.* Translated and edited by Michael Smithies. Kuala Lumpur: Oxford University Press, 1993.

COLLIS, Maurice. *Siamese White.* London: Faber and Faber, 1936.

CRUYSSE, Dirk van der. *Louis XIV et le Siam.* Paris: Fayard, 1991.

HADA, Reiko. "Madame Marie Guimard under the Ayutthaya Dynasty of the Seventeenth Century", *Journal of the Siam Society* 80, pt.1 (1992): 71–73.

HAMILTON, Alexander. *A Scottish Sea Captain in Southeast Asia 1689–1723.* Edited by Michael Smithies. Chiang Mai: Silkworm Books, 1997.

HUTCHINSON, E.W. *1688 Revolution in Siam: The Memoir of Father de Bèze.* Hong Kong: Hong Kong University Press, 1968.

JACQ-HERGOUALC'H, Michel. *Etude historique et critique du livre de Simon de La Loubère 'Du Royaume de Siam'*. Paris: Editions Recherche sur les Civilisations, 1987.

————. *Etude historique de critique du 'Journal du voyage de Siam' de Claude Céberet, Envoyé extraordinaire du Roi en 1687 et 1688*. Paris: L'Harmattan, 1992.

————. *L'Europe et le Siam du XVIe au XVIIIe siècle: Apports Culturels*. Paris: L'Harmattan, 1993.

LANIER, Lucien. *Etude historique sur les relations de la France et du royaume de Siam de 1662 à 1703*. Versailles: Aubert, 1883.

LAUNAY, Adrien, ed. *Histoire de la Mission de Siam—Documents historiques*. 2 vols. Paris: Société des Missions Etrangères, 1920.

LE BLANC, Marcel. *Histoire de la révolution du royaume de Siam arrivée en 1688 et de l'état présent des Indes*. 2 vols. Lyon: Molin, 1692.

MARTIN, François. *Mémoires, 1665–1694*. 3 vols. Paris: Société de l'Histoire des Colonies Françaises, 1931–4.

SMITHIES, Michael. "Robert Challe and Siam". *Journal of the Siam Society* 81, pt.1 (1993): 91–102.

————. "Jacques de Bourges (c.1630–1714) and Siam", *Journal of the Siam Society* 81, pt.2 (1993): 113–129.

————, ed. *The Siamese Memoirs of Count Claude de Forbin 1685–1688*. Chiang Mai: Silkworm Books, 1997.

SOTTAS, Jules. *Histoire de la Compagnie royale des Indes orientales*. Paris: Plon, 1905.

SPORTÈS, Morgan. *Ombres Siamoises*. Paris: Mobius, n.d. [1994].

TACHARD, Guy. *Voyage de Siam des Pères Jésuites envoyés par le Roi aux Indes et à la Chine*. Paris: Seneuze et Horthemels, 1686.

VONGSURAVATANA, Raphaël. *Un jésuite à la cour de Siam*. Paris: France-Empire, 1992.

WYATT, David K. *Thailand: A Short History*. London: Yale University Press, 1984.

INDEX OF PROPER NAMES, PLACES, AND *SHIPS*